FRAGMENTS & FICTIONS

FRAGMENTS & FICTIONS

Workbooks of an Obscure Writer

William Peden

Fragments and Fictions:
Workbooks of an Obscure Writer / William Peden

Library of Congress Cataloging-in-Publication Data

Peden, William Harwood, 1913–
    Fragments and fictions: workbooks of an obscure writer / William Peden.
        p. cm.
    ISBN 0-922820-10-4
    1. Peden, William Harwood, 1913–   Notebooks, sketchbooks, etc.
    I. Title.
PS3566.E256F7 1990
818'.5403–dc20   90-12056
                                                CIP

Cover Art: Kirsten Johnson
Design: Kirsten Johnson
Typesetting: Carl Mar

First Edition
Printed in the United States of America.

Watermark Press, Inc.
149 N. Broadway
Wichita, Kansas 67202

For Miss Peaches
and the two Bobs

PROLOGUE

Did young people take their pleasure when the sea was warm in May?
Balls and masks begun at midnight, burning ever to midday,
When they made up fresh adventures for the morrow, do you say?

—Robert Browning, "A Toccata of Galuppi's"

TABLE OF CONTENTS

I.   Fragments from the Workbooks of an Obscure Writer

II.   Fictions

Coming Together in Alexandria

The Hatchet Man in the Lighthouse

Ellen's Gift

Family Portrait

Across the Hall

The Blue Slipper

Husband and Wife

Cyclops

Boone County Parable

Below Freezing

Main Currents in American Thought

Endangered Species

Dead Bird in the Basement

Lavinia

The Polar Bear in the Ozarks

Excerpts from the Workbooks appeared in
NEW VIRGINIA REVIEW, Nov. 1989, vol. 7.

FRAGMENTS FROM
THE WORKBOOKS OF AN OBSCURE WRITER

"HE TOUCHED ME with dirt! He touched me with dirt!" (Tom told me this; some middle-aged man was screaming this to the theater manager of the Uptown Theater in Columbia, Mo.). Reminded me of an incident at the same theater where I'd taken Sarah (then seven or eight years old) and one of her friends. I was waiting in the lobby; three children, girls, all under twelve, were coming out, one angrily saying to another: "You keep your hands off my tits...you were playing with my tits all the time!" This disturbed me very much.

———

"I AM SAFE in the security of my own strength" (spoken by a religious fanatic who is also a weakling).

———

A HAND THAT SUDDENLY APPEARED on the kitchen wall of our house in Charlottesville while Bessie was doing the ironing, circa 1950.

———————

THE PLEASANT ECCENTRIC at Leonardtown, Maryland (he had written me about something I'd written on Jefferson, and invited us for dinner); a magnificent — but rundown — river mansion. His study was filled with manuscripts stored in liquor cartons. He contended vigorously — after several drinks — that George Washington had six toes on one of his feet. Had a bathtub in which Washington was said to have bathed. Showed it to me. We had a superb lunch, served by his father.

———————

FRED CHAPPELL, curled up sound asleep, on the first pew of the chapel at William Jewell College, where he and I were to conduct workshops, he in poetry, I in fiction: 9:30 a.m.

———————

OPENING FOR A STORY tentatively entitled "Sanding at Midnight": My husband builds things. Our whole house is filled with things he builds. On our wedding night he built our bed.

———————

ANDREW LYTLE'S ANECDOTE about John Crowe Ransom's uncle — or cousin, I can't remember which — who allegedly "would bite the head off a worm for a dime."

———————

THE MIDDLE-AGED COUPLE approaching me one morning at Boulder when, with a bad hangover, I was going to breakfast. Ludicrous: the pale-faced man, skinny white legs hanging out of his shorts; and his wife a portly hausfrau type — metropolitan, big city — both out of place against the background of high sky and mountains...but as they passed me the man was tenderly quoting one of the love quatrains from the *Rubaiyat* and the woman was looking up at him equally tenderly. I felt ashamed of myself, they were wonderful, their image keeps occurring and recurring....

———————

QUESTIONS I HEARD from our kitchen: our daughters, five and eight, to their mother:

"How does the sperm get into the mother?"
"Why wasn't Jesus a lady?"

———————

A DISTINGUISHED-LOOKING white-haired man at the Harvard Club drinking coffee and absent-mindedly stroking his penis.

———————

MARRIED PEOPLE in restaurants, eating and drinking and saying nothing, absolutely nothing; ignoring each other, a pitiful sight.

———————

BRENDAN BEHAN at the Algonquin; we talked briefly in the lobby. He was irritated at the publicity about the New York city fathers' refusal to let him march in the St. Patrick's Day parade (probably because of the incident when Behan allegedly — I did not witness it — turned his back, on stage, to the audience, dropped his pants, and farted). He told me he had just been invited to march in the St. Pat's parade in Boston...and was delighted.

———————

CLIMBING ON A POLICEMAN'S HORSE at the Curls Neck race course, a very rainy day, 1935....how pleasant the police were in those days!

———————

CHARLIE SOMEBODY — (I can't remember his name but his father, I think, was a minister in Roanoke); it is said that the father forbade him to return to Roanoke because of his drinking; indeed, forbade him entry to the family house. One morning I awoke to find him sleeping under my bed in the Delta Tau Delta house, wrapped in a great fur coat.

———————

APPOMATTOX: in 1938 just a grass-overgrown meadow...*sic transit....*

———————

A YOUNGISH WOMAN, in ill health, owns a dog, also in ill health. One day she tells her husband that she thinks there is a parallel between herself and the dog: when the dog feels good, she feels good, and vice versa. Finally the idea becomes obsessive, she begins to believe this self-created myth. The dog becomes sicker, finally runs away, is run over by an automobile. What next? What will happen to the woman?

———————

"ARE YOU AFRAID of a dead bird?" One seven-year-old boy to another at the country club pool one Sunday as I lay in the water recovering from a hangover.

———————

A COLLEGE PROFESSOR, naked, being chased through his own house by the wife – also naked – of the chased man's colleague, a distinguished Renaissance scholar.

———

MAN IS IN PSYCHIATRIC WARD of a big medical center where his wife is a patient. A young girl – also a patient – late teens or early twenties, quietly enters the room (wife is asleep, man is sitting on chair by side of the bed) and after hesitation, looking at the sleeping wife, shyly asks:
   "Are you her husband?"
   He replies, "Yes."
   Girl hesitates again, then asks: "Do you mind if I pray for her?"
   Man starts to say "that would be very nice" or something of that sort when a nurse enters and brusquely leads the young girl away….At the time the man thinks the patient's prayer might have been of more value than all the nurses and doctors in the world.

———

A MAN – a bachelor – listening to an open-air park concert, sticks out his foot and deliberately trips up a running child.

———

A LEADING CITIZEN in a town like Charlottesville, drunk at an auction, buys hundreds of boxes of Kotex for his wife, but she, having passed the menopause, has no use for them...so he gives them to his mistress.

———————

A STRING OF SILVER FOIL from a Christmas tree, dangling from a newly-leafed tree in late spring; conversely, a garden chair on a snow-covered patio.

———————

A GROUP OF PEOPLE, typical middle-class, assembled at a park before a band concert...children playing on swings...basket suppers...as always, some child falls and skins his knee, or drops an ice cream cone and starts howling, &c&c&c; husbands sitting on blankets with wives, it is dusk; hill to left, half-obscured by gathering darkness, trees, &c...children are in play area, beyond the trees...suddenly one child emerges, screaming, face bloodied, followed by another until a horde of children appear, screaming, bloodied....what has caused this terror?

———————

MAN EXPLAINING possible step-mother to a dubious daughter: "we have a lot in common...we both drink too much."

———————

"I DUG HIS GRAVE with a silver spade/And I put him down with a golden chain/Saying goodbye, Old Blue, I'll be coming too." Good title: Dig My Grave with a Silver Spade.

———————

I WOULD WALK through fire and water for that woman — preferably water.

———————

LOOKING BACK over the twenty-eight years as a Virginia school teacher, I wonder, what does it all amount to? I have made a scanty living which had to be shared with my family. There is no money saved except what has gone into the retirement fund, and that does not amount to much for a teacher with a salary as low as mine. It has been a life of doing for others, either family or school. Has it been worth while? I do not know. Two of my friends went to Washington and worked for salaries several times the size of mine, married, and are considered successful women. Both say they wish they had remained school teachers. I do not know. (letter sent me Nov. 1946, writer born 1896).

———————

ON A FISHING TRIP, alone, a man, high in the Colorado Rockies, breaks a crust of ice for a drink; the face in the water of the lake is not his own.

———————

"WHO THE HELL are *you*?" man waking up in bed with a woman he loves.

———————

DETAIL FOR A STORY: wife, after argument, proffers her hand in a gesture of reconciliation; husband pours hot coffee on it.

———————

DETAIL FOR ENDING A STORY: man is walking his dog late at night. Respectable middle-class neighborhood....suddenly, unaccountably, he is frightened, starts running, faster and faster, madly....

———————

MINOR BUT NICE EPHIPHANY: use in story or *as* story: narrator is, say, in a subway station, bus depot, or some public, semi-disreputable place. Narrator, a writer, watching people, feels contemptuous about a youngish man, stevedore or something, heavy, even brutish face. A young woman, university student type, well-dressed, faints, falls down, her skirt in disarray, legs, thighs, panties exposed....the brutish-looking man kneels beside her, instinctively lowering and re-arranging her skirt. Narrator is properly chastened by this — is the phrase Wordsworth's? — "little act of kindness or of love."

———————

"TESS IS a transistional {*sic*} figure with a disadvantage at either end." English novel exam, 1974.

———————

GEORGE PACE told me he knew a man in South Carolina with the Lord's Prayer engraved on his gold tooth.

———————

A PROFESSOR in the lounge of the faculty club at Princeton, drinking coffee — at 9:30 a.m. — with colleagues, comments sadly: "It's been a long, long day."

———————

FROM A CONVERSATION with Erskine Caldwell, circa 1968:
He said he loved dictionaries — except the 3rd Webster International which he gave away....Sherwood Anderson is the short story writer whom he most admires, and has throughout his entire career.... He writes every day, nine months a year, and spends the other three in travel....Writes with the shades pulled down, winter or summer... "The short story *the* perfect form but in bad shape because of shrinking market...." Is paid in

rubles for sale of his books in Russia, but can't take money out of the country..."I'm just a story teller..., I wouldn't want to make my living any other way....If you're not writing for yourself, you're just a hack....There's *everything* to write about." When I asked him what writer influenced him most when he was getting started, he replied: "The written word." To question of would he write as many novels as short stories if he started over, he said he "would have written more, but you don't recognize your limitations till it's too late; this is one of the sad things."

———

GOOD NAME for a dog: Sweetie Low-born.

———

DYLAN THOMAS lamenting (with curses) about women, on our porch, two A.M., shortly after Caitlin had savagely smote one of my colleagues in the belly.

———

AN OVERTURNED tumbler of spring wild flowers left at the foot of a tree by a frightened child

———

THE *FEELING*, not the sound (not so palpable as a sound, though definitely very *real*) of a dog rushing by my bedroom window one midnight; this was repeated the following night. Very unnerving.

———————

A KAFKAESQUE STORY — realism/fantasy — of a father who every morning sets his son off on a backbreaking and spirit-crushing task, all of them meaningless, and yet the father loves the child and is not a sadist.

———————

GOOD NAME for a family pet: Old Balls

———————

JAMES BALDWIN describing his trips to Alabama for *Esquire*, in my room at the writers' conference at some college in Staten Island (Dick Wathen, one of the angels for *Story*, was also there).

His description of his "dilemma," a closet subject in those days....Saw him years later at the National Book Awards, with Norman Macleod's brother, wearing a great chinchilla or caracul hat almost as tall as he was.

———————

A MAN sitting with his feet up on a chair or an ottoman; his wife sits down on them; his legs snap like chalk (that's why they call him Chalky)

———————

A MAN has been taking a sunbath on his patio or deck...dressing hurriedly, he leaves his trunks and jockstrap on the bedroom floor; returning later that night after a bad time with some woman, he discovers a dead spider in the jockstrap. This unnerves him greatly

———————

A MAN who deliberately drops his grandfather's gold watch into a mason jar full of corn whiskey

———————

SOME GREAT ACTUAL INCIDENTS:
   The lion I saw, with a man, walking down College Avenue, College Park...later I could not believe this, but it actually occurred.
   An elderly woman, in an old but well-taken-care-of limousine, liveried chauffer; and in the back seat beside her, a goat.
   Elephants in the Blue Ridge, some ten–twenty miles from Staunton when we — Thorton Terhune, Jack Sirich and I — were coming back to Charlottesville from Cow Pasture...about 3 a.m. We thought we were hallucinating — very high and had half-rolled, half-tumbled, down the

mountain. The next day we read that the elephants were from a travelling circus.

The strange cry I heard one midnight while walking past the reflecting pool by the University of Virginia gymnasium (in more recent years, the pool has been filled up).

The mad dog that followed us home to Bob Black's house, Thomson Road.

The old roué — marcelled white hair, Micawber nose, tan double-breasted camel's hair coat — who approached me as I left the liquor store near the National Theater; looked at me viciously and said, "Why, you goddamned nogood son of a bitch!"

———

"I'LL TELL you what...you're not going to see me studying just to stay out of the army" (student conversation circa 1960).

———

MAN IN A BAR — I don't remember where or when — bothered by a barfly, says: "Fly away home, Jack."

———

SANTA MARIA, CALIF (AP)

"Why Patricia Rush screamed and died as her sister died four years ago may never be known.

'They'll never find out what caused it,' said Everett Stephens, the dead woman's father.

Dr. John P. Blanchard, Santa Barbara's autopsy surgeon, agreed: 'In all probability, the girl's father is right.' He ruled the death came from natural but undetermined causes.

The 23-year-old woman awoke early Wednesday, gave a piercing scream, and died. Mrs. Rush's sister, Beverly Stephens, 17, emerged from a swimming pool in 1963, looked around horrified, screamed and died.

Stephens and his wife say they are now concerned for the welfare of their other two daughters, aged 17 and 11."

———

DON'T EXPECT ME to sit home darning your sox and washing your dirty underwear while you go whoring all over Boone County...overheard in a bar somewhere, can't remember where.

———

A WOMAN who separates — it will be permanent — from a man she has lived with and admired for years, leaving him only an Edith Piaf record.

———

FOCKINK: (name of a gin in bar at the Parador in Javea)

––––––––

NELSON ALGREN'S wife (a very pleasant woman, I think her name was Amanda) passing out at their house in Gary, Indiana, after a huge and delicious day-after-Christmas dinner and many drinks. There is a small pond a hundred yards or so from their house where Nelson keeps a rowboat "for exercise." One of his friends, a drug pusher, drove me from the house to elevated train to Chicago. Amanda had said Nelson would get in trouble because of the drug pushing.

––––––––

"SHARE THE WEALTH," woman to husband who turns his back as he takes off his shorts.

"Share the poverty, you mean," he replies.

––––––––

THE FEAR of open spaces...Pip in *Moby Dick*...swimming one night when the moon rose and the water suddenly turned cold: terror. Similarly once as a child, sitting on the roof of our garage, watching Mars; suddenly wanted to rush inside with the family.

––––––––

STORY OF A MAN who each morning, awakening and looking at the emptiness of his bed, mutters, "the salt has lost its savor."

––––––––––

LIFE COPYING ART: Haldeen Braddy brought me an unopened bottle of beer he had found stashed in the tank of a toilet in their motel (*The Lost Weekend*).

––––––––––

BREAKFAST WITH BORGES and his wife in coffee shop at LaSalle Hotel, Chicago. He was very gentle, soft-spoken, but animated (the marriage did not last long, but she was with him when they visited us in Columbia a couple of years later). Extreme concentration with which Borges ate: an absolutely dedicated concentration (not unlike Carlos Fuentes drinking orange juice or cutting his fish). He delivered a marvelous monologue on Mark Twain; very fond of *Huck*; does not think much of *Tom Sawyer*. Was pleased that I had included "The Circular Ruins" in *29 Stories*. Lamented to Miss Peaches the practices of some of his translators; specifically mentioned the "mistranslation" of *oscura*, and translators' "manhandling cognates."

––––––––––

HALLOWEEN IN NORFOLK, sometime in Sixties: a young black boy dressed like a white rabbit...children selling paper masks made from newspaper: two cents.

———————

"THE HEAD was aten off but the body [of a grasshopper] was walking around." Sarah, 10 July, 1954.

———————

"I'LL BUY IT but I'll be damned if I'll drink it," Dean Emeritus Taliaferro (University of Maryland) concerning a villainous looking mint julep served him at a bar.

———————

LIVING IN a kind of venereal twilight

———————

A YOUNG WOMAN who sleeps with her professor but cannot bring herself to address him by his first name

———————

"TIRED LITTLE SHOES": a child's muddy shoes at the foot of the stairs one night...which in turn made me think of my own children when they were very young....Ellen as a child wore out shoes quicker than I could imagine possible.

––––––––––

TWO PARAPLEGICS, each in own wheelchair, a boy and a girl, sitting in the sun outside the Arts and Science Building, holding hands....how very nice that was!

––––––––––

AS LONELY AS the solitary child dressed up as a spook, trick-or-treating on Mackland Drive, Albuquerque, a very cold Halloween, 1956

––––––––––

A BAR IN SAN FRANCISCO, at a time "the Swim" was popular, where dwarfs grotesquely danced with giantesses...not unlike the even-more grotesque bar in Gaslight Square (now abolished) where the "act" consisted of the most hideous female dwarf in the world singing and being stroked {rubbed} &c by an equally hideous giantess

––––––––––

HALLIE B, for reasons unknown to me, saying I had "sold out" to Martha Foley...she was upset because some Jamaican was pursuing Annie [Burnett] at the College Story contest cocktail party. At same party some woman publicity director referred to Spelvin's critical work as a "classic"...Mary Lou Williams, eyes closed, playing at the Hickory House.

———

A NOTE GIVEN to me surreptitiously half a century ago by a young woman inmate at State Hospital Number 1 (Staunton) — then simply referred to as the insane asylum: "Please write to my brother and tell him I said to come after me at once that I am in a very dangerous ward. His address is Talbott Avenue, Norfok, Va. I am his sister only 23 years old and crave a life of freedom at once" (written on a page torn from some woman's magazines; I still have it)

———

TWO GENTEEL LITTLE OLD LADIES having lunch at the City Art Museum, St. Louis. A group of four or five girls and two boys, all teenagers, wearing very tight shorts or faded jeans; after an unsuccessful attempt to find a table, they departed noisily. One old lady, sipping her martini, observed: "*That's* part of the Great Society."

———

A MAN who before going to bed with a lover (a new one) calls bellboy to bring him a glass of water "for his dentures"; he doesn't actually have false teeth. Ha-ha-ha

———————

SARAH, aged seven, full of talk about God. Says she is "going in" for "book writing" when she's a little older; title of first one will be "My Curiosities." Wanted to know how many pages a book should have, and wonders whether or not people would read it. Has decided on a blue cover with white lettering.

———————

JIMMY FARRELL complaining about his football knee and playing with his toes at the Tiger Hotel, Columbia, Mo., 1948.

———————

MARY MCCARTHY told me a story about Paul Bowles having been ravished by Arabs. She looked beautiful and was wearing a handsome dress which she said her brother Kevin had designed.

———————

A MINISTER in a French restaurant in Princeton where Adrienne and I were having dinner, overheard during a sudden lull in the conversation: "I have as much culture as any of those professors at the University."

———————

"ARE YOU HER ANTHONY tonight?" boy to a man dating his divorced mother.

———————

BEETS COOKING smell like fresh earth

———————

A HALF-ASSED SCHOLAR who spends years writing a biography of the Archbishop of Canterbury — in Chaucerian English

———————

"GUNS AND VIOLINS REPAIRED": sign on an isolated barn in Ohio, driving with Paul Kendall, Athens to Columbus, November, 1962.

———————

"...FOR SOON WE'LL HAVE/ a lonely night for sleeping, and that's forever." Asklepeides (from the *Greek Anthology*, Dudley Fitts' translation).

————————

THE MORNING I awakened to look directly into the snarling face of a stuffed leopard one of my fraternity brothers had temporarily "borrowed" from the zoological museum (Brooks Hall); another morning, I found an amputated penis beneath my pillow (typical "prank" of fraternity brothers who were first year medical students).

————————

"THE WIND is full of ghosts tonight." Garland Ross's, now dead, alas, favorite line (from Millay's sonnet); we used to paraphrase it as "the ghosts are full of wind tonight"; we thought this was terribly funny.

————————

THE DISTINGUISHED SEXOLOGIST (co-author of a huge book on sexual behavior that Whit Burnett/Hawthorne Books had just published) who, in effect, crashed our party at the Algonquin, went mad over the young woman (later I came to know her quite well) into whose beautiful and exposed bosom he was constantly peering; he, late that evening, broke his leg falling down the very steep flight of stairs beyond the bar (all this after an earlier, more sedate cocktail party given by Hawthorne Books).

THE INDIANS in Taos, a cold morning after Christmas — magnificent day, mountains covered with snow — all of them with Montgomery Ward-type blankets slung over their shoulders.

Visited the graves of Freda and D.H. Lawrence, accompanied by Angie (Italian ex-World War I pilot and, of course, Freda's lover); took us to the lower ranch, filled with D.H.'s paintings...I guess they're in a museum now...there were flowers on the grave...somewhere there is a snapshot I took.

ALLEN SEAGER frequently looking at himself in the mirror of our (Drummond, McAfee, my) motel in Iowa City; a torrential talker and, I felt, not really a terribly nice person.

THE FIRST TIME I met Katherine Anne Porter (cocktail party given by Adrienne, Washington, D.C.) I did not recognize her; I thought she was a beautiful but rather silly grandmotherly type who talked primarily — and very pleasantly — about the Pedens she had known in Texas. Similarly Caroline Gordon, at a cocktail party at Norman and Vivienne's, had talked with me basically about the *sounds* of the titles of her books (she had just finished *The Women on the Porch*, and loved the *sound* of it). A neat, pleasant little woman with flashing black eyes...she became stouter later. Allen very much a dude, and very pleasant, and a "womanizer" (Carlos Baker's phrase).

———

TIME WITH GREEN WYRICK, walking near bluffs along the Missouri River; peered into a cave. A pair of students are fornicating: we beat a hasty retreat. Have a couple of drinks on bluff overlooking the River: beautiful. On way back, we pass the same cave: two or three farmers are on hands and knees peeping into the cave while we are peeping at them; title "Susanna and the Farmers," or "The Peepers Peeped Upon"?

———

A DAUGHTER who breaks up a new car — deliberately? subconscious wish? — the night after her father had brought a woman she disliked to the house for a drink

———

PAUL KENDALL told me this: a student's written excuse for having missed a 10-minute quiz the week before: Dear Professor: Last week I had to have my ovaries scraped and was therefore unable to take your quiz.

———————

A HUSBAND who does sitting-up exercises in bed; this eventually drives his wife into frenzies of irritation, culminating in divorce

———————

SUPPOSE A WOMAN, boiling a chicken, takes the whole savory carcas from the pot, and suddenly it emits a terrible scream

———————

"CAPTAIN QUEEG, with his steel balls, is an intriguing person." From an essay submitted in the annual Friends of the [Missouri] Library competition.

———————

TREES AS GRAVE and unyielding as middle-class Englishmen at a funeral

———————

LINE IN A LETTER from a man to his lover; "Where you are, my darling, the leaves must be falling; here, alas, the very trees are falling."

———————

A WRITER who can't get started in the morning until the mail arrives; if he receives no rejection slip that day he feels, somehow, that he's been granted a reprieve, and he gets down to work

———————

THERE'S MANY a limp prick nestled in a pair of Bill Blass slacks.

———————

AN OLD BIRD [penis] should remain quietly in his nest

———————

THE HORROR on the face of a five-year old boy in the grocery store in College Park, seeing — for the first time, I assume — a dead fish, displayed, as was the custom in those days, in a great glass-enclosed bin of cracked ice. I tried to do a painting of this.

———————

A COLLEAGUE'S five-year old son asking me to "make it [a dead bird] go"; fell apart when I told him it was impossible

---

POEM FOR AN OLD MAN: New Orleans, AWP meetings. Dinner at St. Mary Dominican: buffet, we're eating with a translator and his wife; suddenly wild and terrible jungle cries, like the screeching of macaws and innumerable monkeys screaming at each other. Turns out to be coming from a tiny, bearded, black-clad little man I'd met earlier (after my reading, I think). I go to his table, tell him to knock it off or something. No animosity: turns out that one of his table companions had been a student of mine at North Carolina-Greensboro. We end with many abrazos and as I leave to return to our own table the Toulouse-Lautrec type embraces me, tells me he's going "to write a poem to an old man."

A WOMAN whose skin looks as though, if pinched, a few drops of sour milk would emerge

---

AT FORTY, one is more impressed by the fact that there has to be a last time than that there ever had been a first time.

THE LONE HORN in the first movement of Beethoven's Ninth, alone and clear just before being engulfed by tremendous chords of destruction: symbol of 20th century man?????

"THEY FLEE FROM ME that somtyme did me seke/ With naked foote stalking within my chambre./ I have seen them gentil tame and meke/ That now are wyld and do not remembre....(Wyatt, "The Lover Forsaken...")

"NOT IN UTTER NAKEDNESS/ Not in Entire Forgetfulness"; good title??? Wordsworth Ode, of course.

BAR IN THE BAHAMAS, middle-aged woman playing, time and time again, "If I had my life to live over."

THE NIGHT the hogs screamed: had driven to St. Louis to pick up Carlos Fuentes (in those days he refused to travel by air). Violent snow storm, so we stopped at motel in Wentzville. All night a truckload of hogs were screaming, apparently in agony at the sub-zero weather.

TERRIBLE SIGHTS: buttocks of fat girls like two sacks of drowning kittens; a hipster student I saw at some university, with a wax banana in her mouth

---

STORY POSSIBILITY: the two Spanish (or perhaps Mexican) brothers, aged around eight and four, playing "assassin" at the Holiday Inn pool in Freeport-Lucaya...obviously detested each other. Their sister spat great triumphant streams of water at the younger brother — Corky — who had just bitten her and been soundly spanked by the grandmother. Later Corky disappeared; there was fear he had gone to the sea and drowned; search party active; shortly after, he returned, triumphant at being the center of things.

COPULATING HOGS on the way to the slaughterhouse

STORY ABOUT cutting down the pinetrees on Maywood Lane, seen through the eyes of a child, Mrs. Mathew a gentlewoman, shoots the woman who had, at night, been vandalizing the trees; her final — and in those years and in that place the ultimate-threat, though, was "I'll sell [her house] to Nigras." circa 1940

———————

A DRUNK who signs hotel register as S. Agonistes

———————

A FATHER WHO, alternately, nicknames his daughter Scrooge, Rock of Ages, Picasso...when he wants to be left alone he gently but firmly asks her to go practice her flute lessons

———————

GOOD NAMES for music combos: Paul Gaugin and the Five Lepers; The Ticks; Baby Peggy and the Abortionists

———————

ODD THINGS I have seen or heard: Jack Dalton addressing the waitress in a greasy-spoon sort of place between Charlottesville and Washington: "Ha, wha' ya' going', ya crawlin' ferlie"? (from Burns' "To a Louse").

A waitress in a hotel in Durham complaining that people were being hateful to her, and that people shouldn't be hateful to each other.

A taxicab driver in Washington, D.C., who told me that everything he had touched that day had "turned to shit."

George P. Elliott's wife telling me in their kitchen, while an uproar raged in the living room, about George's desire to buy a human skull, and that he had finally bought one, his most-prized possession.

Vance Bourjailly's wife, quite drunk, raging to me about Martha Foley...Vance a very jealous man and a terribly nice person.

Ward Dorrance in despair and defiance pulling down great swatches of wallpaper from the ceiling at Confederate Hill after we had been quietly drinking all evening.

Adrienne striking Denis Devlin savagely after she and Vivienne crashed the stag party — around midnight — at Denis's apartment (Denis, myself, Norman Macleod, Allen Tate, and Lon Cheny).

Sarah talking about "spinners" and "thunderscads" while we were driving through Goshen Pass.

Tom McAfee brutally cursing Don Drummond at a motel in Iowa City after the *Esquire* soiree.

———

DON'T SEND my boy to Harvard,
    The dying mother said;
    Don't send my boy to Illinois,
    I'd rather see him dead.
    But send him to Virginia,

I know that he'll do well;
And rather than to W. and L.,
I'd send my boy to hell.

MAIDIE D., star of the Virginia Players and a thoroughly nice person, clad in red pajamas on a cold winter night in Charlottesville, swinging drunkenly from the bell-chapel tower rope at the University chapel. (Dead now, perhaps? I hope not.) We had chased her from the Delta Tau Delta house to the chapel, she running like a deer. Later, I believe it was she who pursued Ben Belitt, he chastely retreating, and allegedly once broke into his room in the middle of the night, threatening him with a pistol if he would not make love....He didn't.

WARD'S ADMITTING to me (what I had known, of course) that for years he had had an insane love affair with a house.

INCIDENT INVOLVING BILLY H., a good friend from Washington and Lee (visiting professor at Charlottesville one summer), tipsily reading a newspaper upside down, at midnight, in the common room; I bade him goodnight, he swaying in his chair. In my room, I soon heard cries of *Good God, Good God*, and sounds of a hasty retreat. Much excitement next morning; the housemen had found a huge possum in Billy's bathroom, and were having great fun removing it from the Club; a great lump of fat flesh, drooling long strings of mucus...it was this benevolent monster that had affrighted Billy the preceding night.

I HEARD THIS ON T.V. A twenty-year old co-ed at Arizona State shot and killed herself in the desert outside Tempe. Her father — because she had a date with a married man — had told her she had to shoot her pet mongrel dog. He drove her, with gun and dog, to the desert...and she shot herself instead. Ugh.

A YOUNG WOMAN who took the copy of Shelley out of my bookcase in the fraternity house and read aloud "Hail to thee, blythe spirit," &c., pronouncing it *blith*....I never saw her again, for various reasons.

ANOTHER YOUNG WOMAN, minor actress — also in Delta Tau Delta House — telling me, jokingly I thought, that the events of that day would send her to the Lady of the Lake Convent in San Antone...I never saw her again, though five days later I received a card from her, in San Antone, with a picture of the convent...and the note saying I had sent her there. She was really one of the lost and destroyed ones of the Thirties, incredibly beautiful (Winchell had hailed her as a coming star) but with the morals of an amoeba. Her sister worked in the University library, and was a model of propriety.

MY CLOSE FRIEND HARRY when we were children, 6–7 years old. One St. Patrick's Day I showed him a St. Patrick's card I had just received from an aunt, a harp of shamrocks or something of the sort, then, carelessly, unthinkingly, tossed it upon a table, and it fell to the floor. Livid, Harry retrieved it and flew at me screaming, "you goddamned bloody Henglish-man!"

A MAN who always pops a cough drop into his mouth before lighting a cigarette and once, talking in class with a cigarette in his mouth, absent-mindedly puts in a second cigarette and starts to light it

---

SOME JOKER sitting next to Tom and me at local hotel describing his "loved one" to a companion; "perfectly-formed lips," "adorable little hands," et al. "Go placidly amid the noise & haste, & remember what peace there may be in silence."

THE GERMANS at the parador in Javea bug me (the Spaniards I love...and we are the only Americans...for all six weeks). One particularly obnoxious couple stare at Miss Peaches as though she were a creature from another planet. When they have a table across from ours, I threaten to make obscene gestures: the single fork, the double fork, the copulation sign, or Ernst Braun's technique of simply leaning forward, removing his glasses, and staring fixedly at the center of one breast, eventually focusing on the nipple if available.

———

NAME OF A DEAN for a burlesque university story: Dean Gunga

———

THE RATHER PRISSY but not obnoxious school teacher, middle-aged, who fell into the swimming pool at the Chorrillo on her way to the Casa Grande for dinner...poor soul had apparently been having a snifter in her room. She left early the next day, though she had planned to stay longer

———

RICHARD THE CHICKEN-HEARTED: Senator Humphrey's term for Richard Nixon

———

ANYBODY WHO writes a story about anybody writing a story should be shot (see "Introduction" to Penguin edition of *Tristram Shandy*)

———

INCREDIBLE production of *Troilus and Cressida* at the new Shakespeare Theatre in Stratford (Sept. 1968...we went with Kadi); Thersites, for example, was covered with the most grotesque sores and possessed an enormous phallus which was curled between his legs and up to the small of his back; eventually, as final holocaust approached, he used it to beat a drum. Achilles was portrayed as an androgyne and Hector as a Negro...C.P. and Lady Snow sat directly behind us.

———

"CANDLEFLIES," Aunt Lovie once said, gave her a "beeled" ear. Other family malapropisms: blue bonnet plague; tergmont; cockerel spaniel; a porched egg; cholera morbus.

———

DRIVING TO LEXINGTON with Sarah, then about ten, happened to recall the time I took Ellen, then five or six, and our first Christmas in Missouri, on bus (we had no car then) to see the Christmas decorations; she fell asleep on the way home. Sarah reflected a bit, said, "how sweet," and, after more reflection, added, "and how Missourian."

A VERY ELDERLY — 90, if a day — country woman at the eye specialist's waiting room, muttering, quite audibly, "a little hug, a little kiss, a little pinch on the behind"

a fine-looking old man — also pushing 90, and seemingly a professional man (in Dr. Tinsley's office) — to a middle-aged lady: "Look who you run into when you haven't got your gun!"

"INDEED, we are but shadows." Hawthorne to Sophia Peabody.

"SNOW FLEERIES" our maid, 1967; baked us a "century cake" for Christmas; when Miss Peaches asked her what a century cake was, she said it was baked from a recipe in her family that had come down through the centuries

---

THE YOUNGER of two sisters who always hides the last piece of a jigsaw puzzle in her pony tail; this drives the older sister up the wall

———————

A NICE SCENE: a group of nuns, on a snowy morning, playing volley ball in St. Charles, Missouri

———————

AN EPISODE in a story in which people over forty are allowed use of a country club swimming pool on certain times only, so as not to offend aesthetically the younger members with good bodies

———————

JAY GOULD'S DAUGHTER said just before she died
    Papa, fix the blinds so the bums can't ride;
    If ride they must, let them ride the rods;
    Let them put their trust in the hands of God

———————

CHARACTER in a story known as "Nipples"

———————

FIVE OF THE SILLIEST WORDS in English poetry: "oh splendid and sterile Dolores" (Swinburne)

———

THE MASON JAR of bootleg peach brandy I left in my room; when I returned from Christmas vacation, it had solidified

———

PROTAGONIST of a story: drinks because he's tired, and gets tired because he drinks. Eventually starts seeing things that are not there. "I got tired twenty years ago," he finally tells his psychiatrist "terribly tired"

———

A MAN who refers to his penis as though it were alive, talks to it, &c.

———

STORY IN London *Times*. June, 1982, about the "discovery" of a man in his apartment who had been dead for *seven* years; when neighbors were asked by police why they hadn't noticed not seeing him, their reply was that they thought he'd "been off on holiday."

———

READING THE BALLAD of Robin Hood to Ellen, age six: when I came to the part where Robin, dying, weakly shoots an arrow to mark his burial place, she laid her head on the table and wept.

A DOG who aspires to be a cross country runner: good story possibility?

"MOTHER OF STONE, spume of condors/ High reef of the human dawn/ Spade lost in the primal sand" (*Heights of Macchu Pichu*, Felstiner)

SNOW-SHOE Trips: "Snoe [sic] shoe trips may be made in winter by a party of 18–20 to a special point where a chafing-dish supper or hot oysters may be served." From *Three Hundred Things a Bright Girl Can Do*, Lilla E. Kelley, 1903.

ALBEMARLE COUNTY is haunted by the ghosts of ancestor worship; here reverence for the past approximates neurosis: "Foots" Barclay, a local historian.

A CHARACTER who is constantly smiling, as though he were listening to heavenly music that only he can hear

———————

A NOBLE BUT SADDENING minor epiphany: walking into Sarah's room (she about ten or eleven at the time); she was sitting on the bed with a bureau drawer in front of her; in doing some "cleaning up," she had found an old doll of hers, and was playing with it idly but fondly, and when she saw me she instinctively covered up the doll. A great and good child.

———————

HARDIN CRAIG'S LINE: "They're gaining on us; they're gaining on us: they're gaining on us."
   "Who?"
   "Why, the goddamned sons of bitches, that's who."

———————

"THOSE COLLEGE TEACHERS are bullshit; they break every rule in the books": two youngish summer school students.

———————

WHEN YOU'RE YOUNG, writing to some woman you're fond of is like sending a basket of fruit to someone who doesn't exist, invalided in an imaginary hospital.

———————

PEOPLE WHO constantly fall up or down stairs...this becomes obsessive, it's bigger than they are....The beautiful little old lady who fell down the steps of the Episcopal Church on Good Friday. She was terribly embarrassed about this

———————

AN ELEPHANT at the St. Louis Zoo, his great sad phallus enmired in the dust

———————

"TO DO a camelia" — Proust, in *Swanns's Way*

———————

THE WOMAN in the shoestore in Charlottesville (Charlie actually saw this). She was wearing newly-bought bi-focals, and quickly pulled her skirt over the bald head of the clerk who was trying on her shoes, thinking the head was her bared legs. Could this drive him off his rocker? Commit suicide, perhaps?

THE FINE OLD MAN who had the room next to mine at Boone County Hospital, grousing to his nurse that "My goddam stomach looks like a map of the United States." We became good friends, though I'm afraid he didn't make it.

"...INVISIBLE EVIL, depraved and bold" — John Crowe Ransome, "Prelude to an Evening"

THE OLD WOMAN in the doctor's office, moaning about "her privates." "Comes the youth only once....The old are *immer allein*," Frieda, our German housekeeper.

THE NURSE, wheeling Charlie at the University of Missouri Medical Center, proudly pointed out her son's deformed foot in an alcohol-filled display jar.

THE COUNTRYMAN Tom told me about when we were driving past a Highway 40 liquor store; came into that liquor store and asked for some "red sody pop." When told there was none he grumbled, grumped, and finally slammed out of the door yelling he'd never heard of a place that didn't sell red sody pop, what the hell was going on....

———————

CHILDREN PLAYING at drowning (Columbia Country Club pool)

———————

CATHERINE CANADAY told me this, and swears it is true: a boy in Charlottesville, taken to Monticello for the first time; after seeing the Jefferson tombstone, he asked: "But where are the graves of the two thieves?"

———————

A FATHER at the boat-sailing pond in Dublin bending solicitously over a whining five-year old daughter, saying "Don't cry now...you've had a good time, don't you want to come back soon, aren't you having a good time?" AS I WRITE THIS the child is sobbing because the damned boat wouldn't sail, and the father is sadly leading her away from the pond.

———————

A MAN who sends reprints of academic articles to his mistress; the intellectual's [sic] answer to mink stoles, furnished apartments, trips to Bermuda

———

JEROME WEIDMAN'S comment about the unsigned review — as it was then in *Time* and *Newsweek* — as "something unclean," or like a "savage anonymous phone call."

———

DETAIL: man in Colonnade Club, former tennis coach, allegedly kept a golf ball in a corner cupboard to drive away evil spirits

———

"THAT KIPLING MAN sure does write good." Ellen, aged nine.

———

THEY SAY that Arthur is not really dead, that he is merely sleeping in the Welsh hills, that he will return when he is needed....

———

A SUNDAY SCHOOL incident: 9th grade teacher, Methodist church, telling her class that it was no sin to place another book — a novel, for instance — on top of the Bible, as I had been taught and led to believe as an Episcopalian child. To demonstrate, the teacher dropped the Bible on the floor, at which point one of the children vomited. Surely a coincidence, Sarah assured me...but was/is it?

TITLE for a short story: The Name is Foster, Stephen Foster; or, Just a Few More Days for to Tote the Weary Load

---

TWO WOMEN: Told by her doctor after her annual checkup that she had dangerously high blood pressure, a weak heart, failing eyesight, and kidney stones, the patient replied, "Well, as long as I have my health, why worry?" (told me by George Garrett at the Lubbock airport).

Orthopedic Center, Columbia, 1980. Elderly country woman, wheeled in by some kin. Receptionist asked when she was born; she replied she thought "it was around 1980." Later, responding to another inquiry, she said she was "O.K., I guess, just creepin'," and added that she had gone fishing the night before.

THE ELDERLY LADY on her birthday tottering into the bar at the hotel in Jefferson City, accompanied by her chauffeur; the pianist (or maybe he was playing one of those small organs), the bartender, and the waitress all joined in performing ."Home on the Range" for her; apparently an annual custom.

———

IS THERE A STORY in the faculty swimming hour at the University pool??? (much jockeying for lanes, &c.); and the woman professor who told us she could not stand swimming in the same pool (she shuddered and made a terrible grimace) as the repulsive former associate dean who had made passes at her (refused) and then quietly fought her tenure: Title: At the Natatorium.

———

YORK: tea at Newburgh Priory, an enormous manor house being restored by a Captain retired) and Mrs. Wombwell (yes, Wombwell). Had been in his family for centuries, we were told. Some of Oliver Cromwell's remains — including the heart, Mrs. W. told Miss Peaches and me — are in upper reaches of the house, apparently sealed for all time because of the collapse of said upper regions (Cromwell was decapitated, and his remains hidden in Newburgh Priory, at the return of the Stuarts). Mrs. W. did the talking, the Captain remained silent at safe distance, drinking wine....Later we all went to Shandy Hall, which was in process of being restored...great quantities of wine, cheese, biscuits. The official hostess told us some wonderful stories including one of the last tenant of Shandy Hall, a pensioner whose idiot son was some kind of handyman for the Church and whose remains had been found in the cellar (of Shandy Hall) just 4-5 years ago, either from drinking foul wine or being poisoned by fumes from the church furnace which it was his duty to attend....Later I saw Captain Wombwell, quite drunk by this time, being deposited into their limousine by their chauffeur to wait it out for Mrs. Wombwell.

AN ASSISTANT PROFESSOR, a born loser, entertaining head of department and his wife at dinner, begins a ridiculous and somewhat obscene story about the Rover Boys in Prep School; getting high, and out of control, catches the warning glances from his wife, but can't stop, persists....(conclusion, he is not rehired after his first year).

"WHAT A SILLY FOOL I AM/ What a silly fool I am/ What a silly fool I am/ Next time I'll wear my diaphragm". Sung by Virginia Sorenson at Boulder (tune of Love, O Love, O Careless Love).

BEARS TO CONTROL WORLD, MAN SAYS, SHOOTS ONE IN ZOO.

TORONTO, July 10 (UPI) — A man who police said believed bears were going to take over the world shot a 1500 pound Kodiak in the Riverdale zoo today.

Twelve shots were fired into the animal, the largest at the zoo, before it collapsed and died in front of shocked spectators, including many children.

Police arrested Tefik Kari Hysolli and charged him with possession of a dangerous weapon.

One officer said Hysolli told police that he had a fixation about bears and believed he was doing the right thing in shooting the animal. It was the biggest bear he had ever seen, Hysolli said.

––––––––––

THE TERRIBLE GRIM LITTLE MAN at Langston Hughes's lecture, middle Sixties (I had invited Hughes here against the suggestions of some of my colleagues...received some hate telephone calls, and once or twice suspicious-looking people parked their cars in front of our house...no violence, just parked there and sat: coincidence? definitely not) who once or twice during the lecture rose, and I silenced him, and after the lecture (or maybe a reading, I forget) came to the rostrum, buzzing like a wasp, livid with passion about what he called one of Hughes's "atheistic" poems. Earlier, Tom and I and good old Max Baird had taken Hughes to dinner at the Daniel Boone Hotel, one of the first times a Black had been allowed in the dining room....Later, In Kansas City, there was an even more hostile but non-violent reaction, and I crossed a picket line with Langston....

––––––––––

POLONIOUS, 1964: Go to bed with all, but confide in none

———————

I SMELL heartbreak out there, Jack

———————

SPELVIN AT FIFTY: non-writer; occupation, none; education, meager; future, undecided; assets, Episcopalian

———————

CLARENCE, one of the Negroes (they were not called Blacks then) in the class I taught at the Missouri State Penitentiary. Wrote an Easter play on the betrayal of Christ (gave me a copy, neatly typed in black and red) to be produced on Good Friday. Wanted me to attend, sent me an invitation, we talked about this the week before as we were walking down that long long hall that always gave me the willies); he said he was having difficulty getting the costumes — long robes which obviously the warden wouldn't allow...too easy to conceal weapons. I didn't hear from him, thought the performance had been cancelled, didn't go. The Tuesday after Easter I went over as usual: it turned out Clarence had been put in the hole for trying to stab one of the inmates, and the performance of course had been cancelled, and I never saw him again. (Last time I was there the warden told me Clarence had had ten convictions by the time he was ten.) In all my dealing with him, he was gentle, cooperative, &c...

———————

BLOOM'S ACTION, in the Circe episode, of placing his hand over his genitals while taking an oath....

———————

ROBERT PENN WARREN'S contrast (in lecture at Missouri) between writing and typing (the latter in writers like Herman Wouk); extended by a cynic in the audience as the parallel distinction between love and marriage.

———————

D.H. LAWRENCE'S belief about one shedding one's sickness in books is much too facile a generalization...perhaps, even, palpably false; one aggravates one's sicknesses by writing about them?

———————

SEEING HOMER CROY again 1 May 1965: very much the same — red tie, wide-brimmed hat, big smile — as when he'd enthralled Ellen and Sarah with stories about Jesse James

———————

A MAN who, at seventy, writes down a number each morning, each number one larger than the day before...the numbers representing the number of days since his wife's death

———————

GEORGE GARRETT told me this, and somebody had told it to him: Faulkner had always wanted a son, one was still-born (I think Blotner comments that Faulkner held the infant's body in his arms on the way to the burying place); a second had some birth defect but Faulkner, against the doctor's advice, had the infant brought home from the hospital on the day of its birth. Infant became ill that night. Faulkner telephoned the doctor who was operating on an emergency case at the time and could not come, but informed W.F. that he would rush out to the Faulkner's the first moment possible. When he did arrive, the infant had died; and Faulkner, raving, met him at the door and wildly emptied a six-shooter at the doctor, missing him every time.

———————

ANOTHER SAD STORY; a man Miss Peaches and I met in the palatial gardens of the Parador in Javea...told us he was raising beagles in South Carolina, not far from Hilton Head, and was going to try to sneak back various plants for their garden (his wife, he said loved plants, as did their children). Several times urged us to come visit them, be sure to look him up, &c. Told him we *were* planning to come to Hilton Head in a couple of months (we went regularly to visit Miss Peaches's mother). It turned out, of course, that he was not married, had no children, but did have homosexual reputation (this was in middle sixties, before being gay was tolerated....) Hilton Head doyenne told us this when we were having lunch in Sea Pines...her retired General Motors husband was ill with a cold); sometime later, we heard that the man had committed suicide.

––––––––––

THE WONDERFUL WORKING-CLASS IRISHMAN who sat beside us — we were sitting on a bench by one of the fountains in Stephens Green, Dublin — had a paper sack of fried shrimp...kept offering them to us, and we gladly accepted...quite a characteristic act...never met a Dublin Irishman I didn't like.

––––––––––

A WOMAN of whom it might be said that all her brains were in her breasts

———————

RICK, aged seven, concerning his first communion: I asked him if he had any idea of what it was all about. "Yes," he said, "It was when Jesus was having dinner with his friends." "And the wafer?" I asked. "The bad guys," he replied, "were after him, and they didn't have time to cook it."

———————

DETAIL FOR A STORY: one of our colleagues, a rather proper but decent bachelor, visited by aged mother; one of the two cats he owned and treasured killed a snake and placed it upon the mother's bed. Similarly the dog of a very close friend, who was having an affair, attacked the mistress at a party...apparently going to pieces, the same dog — ironically named Precious — defecated upon the floor of the bedroom where the husband had been unfaithful.

———————

IDEA FOR A VERY BRIEF STORY: a man who tends to confuse right and left, up and down; finally, drunk, he is scalded to death while taking a shower (thinks he is turning on cold water)

———————

THE MAN IN MAJORCA, an ageing dude, rents one of the mattresses (which is for sunbathing only but which he thinks is a water mattress); carefully puts it into the pool, gets on, and it slowly sinks with him...he cannot swim, has to be pulled out of the pool by the young English girl with the absolutely unbelievable breasts he has been trying to spark; he refused to come to dinner for a week thereafter.

———

"NEW MATERIAL is added only by new seeing, not by new sights" — V.S. Pritchett. "Everything is done by quietly submitting to what the unconscious brings" — Odilon Redon. "Don't be a victim" — Rimbaud.

———

STORY CONCEPT? a man, married to a pleasant woman, does a great deal of tom-catting because of which his wife divorces him. Now single, with plenty of money, he indulges in many one-night stands; but they are little more than physical couplings, and he begins to yearn for the more quiet pleasures of marriage. But no one will marry him; they'll sleep with him, go off on weekends with him, but they will not marry him: eventually he goes off his rocker??

———

A NEUROTIC GRADUATE STUDENT doing an MA thesis on "street cries in the work of baroque composers" collects vast masses of material, some of which eventually has nothing to do with street cries or baroque composers; when a friend advises her to limit it to England and get on with the writing, she breaks down completely and [factual case, University of Missouri] is confined to an institution.

————

"I SOMETIMES feel as though I were crazy..." Gaugin.

————

QUESTION: "Why do elephants drink?"
    Answer: "To forget."

————

ANGRY FACES in all the newspapers and magazines: where have all the smiling faces gone?

————

OVERHEARD in a fancy night club, 7 Nov 1974, during a sudden lull in the general buzz/hum of conversation: cultivated woman's voice, "Oh, go dunk your penis in a pony of brandy and light it."

————

SARAH'S COMMENT that one of her high school teachers is the kind who would keep pet butterflies.

———

THE MOST BEAUTIFUL CREPE MYRTLE I've ever seen is in the small burying grounds on Gwynn's Island, magnificent; one day I saw a youngish man standing quietly by one of the graves...that would be a good place to be buried, facing the Chesapeake Bay

———

GEORGE GARRETT told me this one, too: when Faulkner was at the University he bought an expensive riding habit, whip, the works, and had his picture taken astride a wooden horse, which he sent to many friends, acquaintances, and people he didn't like, including Bennet Cerf (whom, apparently, he despised, referring to him as Surf...); also, when Faulkner first came to Charlottesville he consciously dressed very badly: beatup shoes, coat with elbows worn out, &c. G.G.'s feeling is that all along his career Faulkner was a kind of comic, pulling people's legs, and so on....

———

"A BAD DAY for itinerant flower vendors": father to daughter, looking out sadly at a rainswept midwinter Missouri landscape.

———

"SWAN LAKE ANTHOLOGY,"...wonderful malapropism, Charlie after tracheostomy.

HORTENSE CALISHER: one of the saddest — and at the same time most beautiful — faces I have ever seen: some kind of hair arrangement – jet black — which seemed to me a yard high. A warm, lovable human being.

W.D. SNODGRASS here to give a lecture; had drinks with him; he was wearing a pair of new shoes, bought (he told me) for the occasion, but they were paining him frightfully. A pleasant, unpretentious young man, and without the high voice I remembered his having had at Iowa

---

THE WINDOW at the end of the long corridor at the Boone County hospital...how many people, desperate, unhappy, afraid, have stood there and looked out?

YET ANOTHER — and, alas, the last — story George Garrett told me when he and Sam Goldwyn, Jr. were here for a preview of *The Young Lovers*. He, George, was in Hollywood, working on the script. Sam invited George to their place to swim after work (to get him overtime, without pay,

George says, but he went anyhow because he wanted a swim). At poolside, the four Goldwyn children, with their governess and boxer dog, come out to say goodnight to Daddy. At this point, Goldwyn's wife, a former actress, comes out in a towering rage, kicks each of the bathrobed children *and* the dog into the pool. Sam, meanwhile, is backstroking up and down the pool (a good swimmer, he had been on the swimming team at Charlottesville). Three of the Goldwyn children cannot swim: one of them, and the dog, sink like stones, to be rescued by George. When it's all over, Sam emerges from pool, and says: "We'll have to get that in a movie some time."

———

THE PATIENT, a countryman, at the University Medical Center, about to be discharged, who tried to sell his bedroom slippers to Dr. Ray, Chief of Staff, for twenty-five cents; failing in this, he attempted to sell them to Charlie.

———

A COLLEGE PROFESSOR who, attempting to write something on the blackboard in his sophomore English class, inevitably starts drawing nudes; finally, he falls apart, quits academic life forever.

———

QUESTION: "What is point-of-view?"

Professor: "What about it?"

Question: "Do you want us to use it?" (verbatim, first day of beginning class in fiction writing)

NAPOLEON BONAPARTE BAREFOOT (son of a physician in Wilmington, N.C.)

AT THE BELLERIVE, after finishing their set, the musicians joined a couple of women at the table next to us; suddenly, in a moment of sudden silence, one of the women was heard to exclaim: "You were so good I had to go to the bathroom!"

"MAMA is not like people." — Ellen, age five.

CHILD — not a Virginian — coming home from school in Williamsburg the first day of school exclaiming with rapture: "Oh, Mother, there are peacocks in the Palace gardens!"

LEE AND JACKSON, our children's rabbits, eventually turned out to be females....

––––––––

"AT THREE O'CLOCK in the morning, a forgotten package has the same tragic importance of a death sentence." F.S.G., *Far Side of Paradise*.

––––––––

A SUNNY DAY, AROUND NOON, I am sitting in my car outside Lee elementary school, waiting for Ellen to come out of class so I can go with her to the annual parents-students spring picnic. As I wait, a rather beatup little car drives up, the driver in his middle-to-late-middle forties. Soon the boy comes out of school, runs to his father. I am impressed with their mutual affection; without being sloppy about it, they seem very very happy to be with each other; apparently they have been looking forward to this....Then Ellen comes out, we go to the picnic, everything is fine. I return to my car to wait for her to get her books and things (this is the last day of school). And just then I see the father and son who had been so happy an hour earlier...the father walking stiffly ahead of the son who lags behind, on his face a look of utmost grief, as has the father; but the boy's face, particularly, is heartbreaking: humiliated and grief-stricken simultaneously....The father keeps looking back and saying something I cannot hear, and then suddenly he reaches out and grasps the boy's arm and twists it savagely and, my recollection is, the boy strikes back, and then his body crumples, absolutely crumples, and each slams into the car, their faces working with grief, and then the father places his head on the steering wheel of the beatup little car, and presumably wept....They are thousands and thousands of miles apart. I cannot forget this, it haunts me, I have tried to make it into a story, but I miss every time.

I HAVE NOTHING,
I owe much,
The rest I leave to the poor.
— John Gay (1685-1732).

IS THERE A STORY, possibly titled "I Want to Go Home," in the news story, 8 or 9 Jan 1978, of a tax accountant in Illinois who murdered — by beating, stabbing, and in some cases amputation — his six children (and also slit the throat of the family dog...then went to Milwaukee and beat up his estranged wife). Apprehended — I saw this on t.v. — all he could say, struggling with tears: "I want to go home." Phew!

Also on t.v. (I think it was "Sixty Minutes") was a sequence involving a terminally-ill (leukemia) mother of three, being visited by her three children and husband, whose words were the same as the murderer's: "I want to go home." Merely thinking of this breaks me up, and reminds me of O. Henry's last words having been taken, quite unrecognized, from the Chelsea (where Tennessee Williams died in 1983) to the hospital: "Turn on the lights, I don't want to go home in the dark."

———

STUDENT CONVERSATION cramming for English exam at the same time hurrying to get downtown to see a movie (Charlottesville):
Question: "Milton." Answer: "Organ voice of England."
Question: "Keats." Answer: "Shadow of a great rock in a weary land."
Question: "Shakespeare." Answer: "Oh, finesse *him*."

———

TOM'S TELLING ME that at the Stephens College production of *Streetcar*, at the scene when Kowalski is about to rape Blanche and she breaks off the top of a beer bottle and holds him off with it, a Stephens student behind him was passionately saying, "Give it to 'er, give it to 'er."

———

CALLING DRUMMOND at the Western Bar in Cloudcroft, and the woman who answered said, "You just hold on and I'll send a little girl down the street to fetch him." One of the nicest things in a long time.

———

"EVEN THE SIMPLEST achievement is miraculous." — Genet.

───────────

"...THE COLLEGE COURSE in creative writing is always delicately subversive...no matter how careful its academic idiom, it must ultimately reduce itself to the aboriginal lawlessness of human activity." From a student paper, June 1956, Albuquerque.

───────────

FANNY HURST at a cocktail party at the Burnett's: very genial and wearing a ring with a diamond the size of a hen's egg....Edna Ferber saying she hadn't read a review of any of her own books in twenty years....a child climbing over the statue of Alice in Central Park asking her father why some of the places on the statue were shining; "because children like you touch them," he said fondly...another child fell into the pond, father leaped in after him, pulled him out, embraced him...then spanked him: God bless them both....a Jewish rabbi reading the Bible...the bums in Bryant Park or passed out in the men's room of the New York Public Library...K.A.P.'s accounting that she'd had four husbands and sixty lovers, to say nothing of one-night stands..seas and banks of azaleas and boxwood at Montrose Park in Georgetown

───────────

JEAN STAFFORD'S comment that to be loved is beautiful but not to be beautiful is not necessarily *not* to be loved...people who knew her when she was young say she was beautiful...when I met her, in the sixties, she still was, but in a ravaged way...I think it was Bud Guthrie who said to me (in Boulder) that a woman who is being loved *and* loving is like a bitch in heat in terms of other men's wanting her.

CHARACTER ET. AL. FOR A STORY: the son of one of our neighbors in Albuquerque; father a good man, a psychiatrist and lover of music, and a good wife who had been a child prodigy but whose soul had been almost absorbed by her unbelievable obesity....The boy was eight years old, and almost every day I took him swimming with me at the university pool. A gentle lad, more Spanish than most Spaniards; had four sisters, all older than he, and had been so loved by them, (in a conventional, not pathological way) that he is at times not sure whether he is a boy or a girl: reads comics while they dress and undress, talk, are constantly feminine.... And occasionally, every two or three weeks perhaps, he will utter a piercing scream – I have heard it, it is harrowing – and at first you feel like laughing but then you feel as though you were laughing at an inscription on a tombstone...and then the boy will utter a piercing wolfgoat cry, and fall to the floor in a virtual coma

----

ACTUAL FACT: airforce captain — time midway WW2 — shacked up with some slightly disreputable (but not a professional whore) woman who finally fled their room in semi-shock: among other things, her inner thighs were scarred — or maybe just singed — from cigarette burns. Her screams brought a bellboy to the room; the captain beat *him* up, reduced the room to a shambles &c. &c. Court-martialled and sentenced for thirty days; interviewed by the press for a comment, his only reply was "It seems a pretty rough penalty for a minor indiscretion."

———

THE SPLENDOR about Joseph Conrad — real honest-to-God nobility of spirit — that animates his *Notes on Life and Letters*

———

THE CHILD in Madrid, age three, at a birthday party....one of the other children blew up a balloon until it burst....the first child started to laugh, could not stop, laughed himself to death. This was carried by the UPI. Three times I have tried to make a story out of it, set variously at Cumberland Lodge, Javea, somewhere else....no good

———

INVASION OF PRIVACY: an academic story, conflict between a decent young assistant professor and a tyrannical chairman...bullied and mistreated (no raises, no promotion, &c.) no future for him (time is

Depression years, few jobs available). Chairman humiliates him whenever possible. The assistant professor's victory, however, finally comes: his wife has a dream which she tells husband immediately. In the dream she was plaiting violets in Chairman's pubic hair....From that time on, the underling has a sense of victory...the chairman forever is doomed in his mind. Could suggest, beneath the comic/burlesque, a minor "under-theme," the terrible tyranny of the sub-conscious; we are all nakedly vulnerable to the onslaught of *others'* dreams about *us*.

———

AMUSING THINGS I have recently seen: none I can think of

———

SIMILARITY between Cheever's "Enormous Radio" and Hawthorne's "Minister's Black Veil" (and others by H.): discovery of evil in others acts as catalyst to characters' agonizing self-awareness of evil in themselves. Subject for an essay???????

———

RETURNING FROM A WALK (along the meadow of the parkway here); a child of about five who was very carefully maneuvering his kiddiecar — or whatever they're called — stopped me, said hello, told me his daddy had just left (actually I'd seen them earlier as I'd been crossing the meadow); "Well, he'll be back soon," I said. We talked a bit longer, and just as I said "goodby," "see you later," or something of the sort, the boy called after me: "My mama's dead," and all I could answer was, "Oh, that's too bad," or something equally inane.

———————

TIME IN POE; the clock, it might be said, is the protagonist of "Masque of the Red Death."

———————

IS THERE A STORY in Marco, our huge poodle, one of the greatest dogs in history...? We had to give him away because of his habit of opening the screen door, running around town, endangering life and limb of many people by running in front of their cars and suddenly sitting down....We gave him away, regretfully, to a black man who, despondent at the death of his wife, had become a heavy drinker, contemplated suicide, the works. Marco rehabilitated him: man moved out of his shabby room, rented a small flat in a housing project, constantly combs and brushes Marco, goes for long walks with him, and allegedly has a dog-sitter to stay with Marco when he (the man) has to go to work (which apparently is relatively seldom). What Marco thinks of all this I cannot say.

———————

ALMOST the most beautiful human being I have ever seen. Walking from our apartment (Wertland Street, Charlottesville) through the section of

Negro shacks, very hot day. On a porch was a black woman, big, large, not actually homely but very plain, holding aloft a naked black baby perhaps a year and a half old, and smiling, oh, how she was smiling, love and joy radiating from her....I made some sort of recognition gesture with my hand, and the woman smiled back...that was all, but it was a great moment....I wish I could write a story about that woman...I can't think of a single really good short story written by a white man about blacks, and that includes all the so-called classics. Idea for an anthology: the black in fiction as seen by white writers.

––––––––––

WITHOUT BEING A RACIST, or a fascist, or what not, there was much truth in the comment James Purdy made to me — say around 1965 — that a Negro or a Jewish author had a much better chance of becoming "in" than a white protestant

––––––––––

MERCEDES, our maid, told us that strange things were going on in Fayette: death by suicide of three young blacks within a week; another black shot himself in the stomach "but there was no blood"; she is afraid to leave house at night...young man would "go after her children..."

––––––––––

"TOM RECOLLECTIONS": turned upon me like a viper once when I told him his poems were too dark; coming over to the house one very cold night, wearing a suit — not an overcoat — over his pajamas; irony when during a visit from George Garrett we took several pictures with George as a remonstrative father warning a wayward son — Tom — from drink....

———————

BEAUTIFUL BUT ALCOHOLIC woman author whose face was like a lovely cup that had been broken and carelessly glued back together

———————

BALANCED VARIETY within a fundamental unity: the classical piano concerto...could be a good description of the short story

———————

DINNER with two people on train from Baltimore to New York...woman beautiful in theatrical way (upswept ash-blond hair, splendid jewelry, magnificent brocaded robe); man a colonel in military intelligence, just retired; we had several drinks, woman began talking about her recent tour, from Yugoslavia-Tokyo-Hong Kong. It developed that she was Eleanor Steber and had met the colonel on the tour, and they had married.

"My life began then," she said quietly, and with no affectation....Later she referred to someone in State Department as a "horse's ass, if you'll pardon the expression."

———

K.A.P. AND THE Argentinian journalist smelling of armpits

———

AUGUST 1967, EPISODE of some people from Chinese Embassy in London attacking some bobbies...while, as order was being restored, a group of working class English spontaneously began singing "Rule, Brittania." Very great moment.

———

"...THE ESSENTIAL part of a work is precisely that which is not expressed" — Gaugin

———

THE TINY LITTLE INDENTURES at the base of an infant's spine, right above the buttocks, are vestigial remains of what a million years ago would have been a tail (one of my children's pediatricians told me this) [So why is Garcia Marquez's pig's tail magical realism?]

———

RIMBAUD: "Don't be a victim."
  Spelvin: "Don't be an emissary."

POE RELATES that Thomas Dunn English would lap milk with his cat, from a saucer.

MARK, aged five, telling me that his brother Eric, aged ten, was sick in bed "with a blood-red throat," and his parents were afraid that, in addition, he had polio *and* cancer.

A FACT: they found Miss Florence (in her fifties) sitting naked, at midnight, on the top row of the Washington and Lee stadium, staring blankly beyond the playing field.

THE ULTIMATE in non-books: publisher saturates reviewers with advance notices, and well before scheduled publication date sends out strikingly-jacketed, beautifully-bound and printed copies. But except for title pages, dedication, and the like, there is absolutely nothing in it...all pages are blank. It becomes a best seller.

"WHEN THE WIND is in your favor, Daredevil Oliver, you may dive.... And may God have mercy on your soul!" (College Park, Maryland, 1940; subsequently I interviewed Daredevil Oliver and his wife).

CERTAIN TITLES, QUOTATIONS from many sources, from Marlon Perkins's "Wild Kingdom," to George Bernard Shaw on Haydn, demand stories the same way that Stevenson says "certain dark gardens call aloud for a murder; certain old houses demand to be haunted; certain coasts are set apart for shipwreck":

So Old, and So Profane
Smiling, the Boy Fell Dead
Dear Dead Women
A Sheltered People's Mirth
Young Hooligans for Christ
The Days Were Not Long Enough
The Farther I go, the Darker It Gets
All the Empty Places You Must Walk
Junk Food at Midnight
The Most Distressful Country

If Tina May Garrett Can Do It, So Can You
Built My Barns and Strung My Fences

———————

MAN SITTING on chair with five-year old daughter on his lap; he has a mousetrap in his hand; child looks at it with horror. Man is laughing, largely through stupidity ("Enlightenment")

———————

"A FILTHY MIND is a perpetual treasure" (from an early Huxley novel)

———————

STORY about a man who thinks the most horrifying sound in the world is a cry for help...night after night, he has the same terrible dream: he is kissing a drowning open-mouthed woman, whose mouth then becomes a sickening smear of corruption. Yet he returns to her again and again. Circe and the swine? The ultimate Calvinistic curse? In either case, eventually he commits suicide

———————

A MAN of Sorrows, and Acquainted with Grief (Book of Isaiah)

———————

MINOR EPIPHANY: a man buys a quart-sized plastic liquor flask to replace the half-pint flask his estranged wife has stolen from him

———

"THERE'S NO SENSE in going further
    'tis the edge of cultivation
    so they said, and I believed them
    broke my land and sowed my crop."

———

A MOTHER who feels her child die in her womb while the father, a highly-respected small town judge, is out giving a speech

———

SCENE: a bar in Fulton, Missouri, (county seat of Calloway County, seceded from Union during War). Noisy, good-natured crowd. One snatch of dialog (as man and woman enter):
    Man (Barfly, around forty, to a lad of, say, fifteen or sixteen): "You'd speak to him when he's with her?"
    Boy: "Why, sure."
    Man: "You used to shave her legs."
    Boy (proudly): "Shit, I never did no sich a thing."

Outside, a boy with gaiters is wheeling a bicycle with a huge dog in the handlebar basket. Sign over door: "Rooms, $2.50 up. Air Conditioned. Clean." (Time: middle 1950s)

———————

ELLEN, age 3 or 4, watching two squirrels cavorting in Aunt Lovie's huge trees: "I expect they're a male and a female, aren't they?"

———————

A DREAM, 27 January 1981: Paul Kendall, as in life. I asked him whether or not he was in anguish at no longer being alive. He seemed both hurt and angry, and then suddenly he was holding aloft a massive candelabrum with numerous lighted candles that suddenly flickered, dimmed; the candelabrum collapsed, and at that moment I awoke...in a cold sweat.

———————

SAW A MAN in a shower room somewhere; a man tattooed with a tiger chasing a rabbit down his back, almost into his anus. Also, I forget where, a young woman with an eye tattooed around her navel

———————

"CHAPLIN BEFORE JESUS!" Crudely-painted sign on a wall near the Bellas Artes, Mexico City, November 1980.

———

A PROFESSOR'S LAMENT: "How can I face life bravely, serenely, now that someone has stolen my truss!"

———

GREAT SPEECH by Congressman "Guinea" Richardson (from Henry County, had been a Republican, but turned Democrat): addressing the Virginia House; a member of the opposition interrupted, and accused him of being a turncoat. He glared at the heckler, and declaimed:

The flowers of forty-eight summers have bloomed upon my path,
The snows of forty-eight winters have whitened on my brow;
I used to be a baby, but I am no baby now:
GO TO HELL, YOU GODDAMN SON OF A BITCH!

———

AS COMMON as pig tracks; as smart as a buggy whip; as cute as a speckled pup

GOOD SYMBOL: a coffin filled with water

———————

TWO VERY ELDERLY country women in Dr. Tinsley's office. The older mutters, "Once you start goin' down hill they can't do nothin' to stop it." Then, abruptly, she glares at the receptionist, and loudly exclaims: "I don't like that young woman settin' up there!"

———————

SINGLE-SCENE STORY: two faculty members (philosophy department). Once close friends, they have become enemies because one's tomcat keeps tormenting the other's female cat; gets to the point that the owner of the female sprays the tomcat with mace, devises Rube Goldberg contraptions to capture it, &c.

———————

A CURSE, engraved on an ancient Assyrian stone tablet: "May nothing new ever happen to you"

———————

A MAN who comments sincerely, after hearing the Black Watch Pipes and Drums: "What *grand* men the Scots are!"

———————

ONE OF THE VERY GOOD PEOPLE: John Cheever. We stopped at a small bar near the Algonquin on the way to Biltmore where he was to participate in a panel discussion. Told me he and Updike had but recently returned from USIA visit to Russia. Large crowd waiting at airport, and they were greeted with many cheers (Russian equivalent of *Viva Cheever! Viva Updike!*) Said he got along with the Russians better than Updike did, because he "drinks more than Updike" (and I gathered he was not overly fond of Updike). A smallish, ruddy, brisk, thoroughly pleasant man (sport jacket, blue button-down collar shirt). Urbane, completely without pretense or pretentiousness. Said he was grateful to the *New Yorker* for having kept him afloat through the years, never dictating to him, &c. &c. &c. Said he liked my reviews of his books. For the first time in his career he had money to do as he wants.... In his subsequent comments at Biltmore, mentioned in passing the "venereal twilight of our age."

———

"TELL IT TO JESUS/ He will carry me home." My grandfather when told he should stop trying to live like a millionaire (as a boy, it seemed to me he did, almost).

———

THE POINT about Jean Stafford is not that she was so physically-ravaged looking, her face lined, her skin of many colors (reddish, blueish, yellowish) but that she has very real inner beauty and graciousness which obliterate the tragic face, the untidy clothes, the messy hair....

———————

A POLAR BEAR at the Forest Park zoo, evidently irritated at the presence of too many noisy spectators, turns his back to them, and defecates. Good metaphor: if you're not overly-concerned with societal "niceties," things aren't going to bug you.

———————

GEORGE ELLIOTT told me that the genesis of *Among the Dangs* was a dream he had when he was at Yaddo....When he stayed with us, he wore a pair of bedroom slippers the shape and color of a bear's foot....

———————

IS IT MORE than coincidence that *Joseph Andrews* was published just a year before the birth of Thomas Jefferson? I doubt it.

———————

A WOMAN who leaves impassioned notes in a man's mailbox after every encounter; this eventually drives him off his rocker and he is carried away screaming

———————

"THE DAYS that make us happy/ make us wise." Quotation from John Masefield; part of a hand-written inscription by Arthur Waugh on the title page of his autobiography (*One Man's World*)

———

A CONTEMPORARY AUTHOR — a kind of 20th century Sisyphus — is on the verge of a nervous breakdown; takes a sea voyage to get away from work, but constantly dreams he's copy-editing the novels of Samuel Richardson, and falls apart.

———

CHILD whose goal is to become a cheerleader...the ultimate 20th century minor folly, her grandfather thinks, and cuts her out of his will

———

A YOUNG DIVORCÉE, spending night in fraternity house with her lover, gives him a crucifix (had been blessed by the Pope when she and her husband were honeymooning in Rome); "I have no need for this where I am going," she says. Three days later he is informed that she has committed suicide.

———

THE NIGHT that Donald Justice caught fire — literally, from leaning against our kitchen stove — after a reading at our university: fortunately, only the suit — made of some new synthetic blend — was damaged

———————

DON'T TRY to tell grandpa how to suck turkey eggs

———————

THE NOISES of Taxco...how different the casa becomes at night! During the day, so alive, so sunny, so cheerful, each of us at our typewriter (I at the large table in the *sala grande*, Miss Peaches in one of the bedrooms); in the kitchen Teresa is humming as she prepares our midday meal. Outside, if the wind is right: music from the *zocolo*; the incessant singing and chirping of many birds; the insane braying of burros and the crowing of roosters (every hour, it seems, some rooster is madly crowing himself to death); the barking or howling of many dogs; the groaning of a lorry laboring up the ascent to the twisting road to Cuernavaca. But when the sun disappears behind the mountains and the air suddenly chills, it becomes a different world. Up here, we are again aware of the presence of the old vengeful gods and the reality of the dark, and it is good when the night watchman knocks at the heavy front door before he lights the baroque lamps, and the gallery and the patio are again warm and golden in their light...

———

"I WOULDN'T think of joining a club that would want me to be a member." Groucho Marx.

———

"IF I HADN'T ALWAYS been so tired, I could have written much better." George Spelvin.

———

ST. AUGUSTINE: "Do not despair; one of the thieves was saved. Do not presume: one of the thieves was damned."

———

SIGN on fence, Boone County, Missouri: Cats Against Intervention in Nicaragua!

———

COMMENTS from the late Bob Thompson, who found these fragments and added his thoughts, as if the writer were not deceased:

A fragment I thought I might find, but didn't. You told me long ago about a conversation you had with someone in Columbia. You were in his den; he was a professional man...possibly a doctor. On his desk was a human skull, which he picked up and told you was from the victim of the last lynching in Boone County (in the 30s or 40s?). He used the skull as an ashtray.

A professor who had a dog that would roll on its back when people approached it. "Can you imagine just exposing yourself like that, to everyone?" he asked a student. I took it as a metaphor for writing. (The professor was you.)

EPILOGUE

"Dust and ashes!" So you creak it, and I want the heart to scold.
Dear, dead women, with such hair, too — what's become of all the gold
Used to hang and brush their bosoms? I feel chilly, and grown old.

— Robert Browning, "A Toccata of Galuppi's"

———————

MINI-FICTIONS

COMING TOGETHER IN ALEXANDRIA
1. The Bridge
2. Fire in the Snow

(*Greensboro Review*)

COMING TOGETHER IN ALEXANDRIA:
THE BRIDGE

IN ALEXANDRIA there are two or three cobblestoned streets, survivors from the Eighteenth Century, that lead straight down to the Potomac River. The Norford is on one of these streets, a tall, narrow mansion-turned-rooming house, close to the sidewalk but extending fifty, maybe seventy-five, feet to a formal brick-walled garden; my bedroom window looks out upon this garden. The window is framed with climbing rosebushes still bearing three or four new buds and many fullblown scarlet beauties; the bushes usually remain in flower until Thanksgiving, now but a few days away. I am tired from the bumpy flight from Atlanta, and lie down to rest; in a moment or two I am asleep and by the time I wake up, shower, and dress it has become as dark as midnight.

To clear my head I decide to walk to the Wise Woman's apartment on Prince Street (I had, of course, called her as soon as I'd arrived at the airport). Formerly the Governor's mansion, the building is now divided into several large suites, a bit shabby but high-ceilinged and still retaining traces of their former grandeur. The adjoining area has become a curious mishmash of expensive dress shops; a fashionable art studio, run by two pleasant young men, lovers, from Chapel Hill; an excellent book store, really first rate; and a small Negro ghetto. At the corner of this ghetto I am confronted by a Negro who suddenly, indeed almost miraculously, emerges from the shadows, approaches me, pauses, swaying slightly; he is about my age and size, I could chin myself on his wine-tainted breath.

"Where is the bridge?" he asks. He has a not unpleasant voice, blurred and slurred from the wine, but not a bad voice; Hampton Institute, I wonder, Howard University?

"What bridge?" I ask. "There are many bridges." I gesture towards Maryland, then towards the District. "The George Mason Memorial? Key Bridge?"

He shakes his head like a wet dog, ponders. "Key Bridge," he says, as much in question as answer.

"Key Bridge." I point in the general direction of the Tidal Basin and the airport. "I was over that bridge a few hours ago. . . . You can get a bus . . . ."

He takes a sudden step towards me. In those days, gone now, alas, I looked upon all Negroes as friends; the thought flashes through my mind *if he has a gun he's got me if it's a knife I can take him . . . .*

"You were just ova' *that* bridge?" His voice is incredulous. "Damn, that's a coincidence, all right."

He sways, shakes his head, tries to focus his eyes. "Now if you read that in a . . . in a O. Henry story, you wooden' believe it . . . . Would you?"

"No, you wouldn't believe it."

He pauses, furtively glances over his shoulder, the dark street is deserted. "Or in a Hemingway story, neither, or one by John Steinbeck." He half-closes his eyes, almost falls off the curb, I reach his elbow to steady him.

"That's right," I say. "No one would believe it." I tell him that I had met Steinbeck once.

"Damn," he says and shakes his head. "That's a coincidence." Again he suddenly steps forward, his breath is like an armed assault, instinctively I raise my left arm. He steps back, points toward the Negro bar and grill I sometimes pass on my way to the Wise Woman's apartment. "Too much to drink," he mutters. "Got to get to the bridge. The pigs are afta' me."

We shake hands, he continues to mutter about getting out of town, the pigs are after him. I fumble for my wallet, all that I have is a twenty and a ten, I push the bills into his hand.

"This will help," I say. "Get a taxi. There's a taxi stand around that corner." He passes the bills from hand to hand, trying to focus his eyes, and then abruptly stuffs them into the pocket of my topcoat.

"Thanks, man," he says. "But no thanks."

"Take them, you can send them back to me some time if you want to, to the Norford here, here in Alexandria." I remove the bills from my pocket, thrust them at him. "Go to that corner, damn you, you can get a cab there."

Fumblingly he tries to give them back. I strike his arm sharply, just above the elbow, you can dislocate a man's elbow that way if you need to. "Please take them," I repeat, smiling, "or I'll break your goddam neck."

He returns a great wide smile. "I appre. . .appresheate that," he says. He shakes my hand, turns and weaves his way to the corner where he stops, looks back at me, and waves. I watch until he disappears around the corner.

Later, half-awake, half-asleep, lying in the Wise Woman's bed and looking bemusedly at the frescoed ceiling, I tell her the story.

"You were very foolish," she says. "And patronizing, too. You can't do that sort of thing any more. You were lucky he didn't knock you over the head, or knife you, or something. That Big White Brother act doesn't play any more."

I snort and close my eyes.

"Nobody walks alone here after dark any more," she says. "It isn't like that any more."

"He was a good man," I say. "I hope he made it to the bridge."

———————

COMING TOGETHER IN ALEXANDRIA:
FIRE IN THE SNOW

"DO YOU REMEMBER the incident in Colorado?" I ask the Wise Woman at breakfast the next morning. "When we were doing our thing at the Colorado Writers' Conference?"

"Which incident?" She puts down her teacup, and smiles. "There were a lot of incidents at *that* conference."

"In the shack. The sheepherder's shack. Someone had driven us there one weekend, someone from the staff . . . I can't recall their names. It was about an hour's drive from Central City . . . maybe a couple of hours. There was this beautiful meadow. Surrounded, of course, by the mountains; you could see the Seven Sisters when you got out of the valley: even the lake, way up there, you could catch a glimpse of it now and then. Flashing in the sun. It was beautiful. And there was this tumble-down shack. Deserted, of course. Falling apart. In a meadow. A sheepherder's shack. The valley was criss-crossed with hoofprints. They must have wintered there."

"I do remember the valley. But the shack? The sheepherder's shack?" She shakes her head.

"You found a sex manual there. A dog-eared paperback. On a shelf with a beatup coffee pot and a bunch of junk, tangled string, a rusty can opener, stuff like that."

The Wise Woman laughs. "Of course, I remember now. How could I forget *that*? The book was falling apart. In that pile of odds and ends on the shelf."

"I wrote a story about it during the summer. Not *about* it, really, but, well, you know, growing *out* of it. The sheepherder was the main character, of course. I tried to get the feeling of what it must have been like for him there . . . , those long, cold nights, the sheep bedded down or moved out to grazing land or shipped off to the slaughterhouse or whatever they do to sheep in the winter. Poor devil, alone in that rickety shack with his sex manual."

"It's a good idea. A very good subject. I'd like to see the story."

"It's just come out," I said. "I haven't actually seen it, it was published while I was away on sabbatical. There'll be copies of it in my office, I should think. I'll bring one over tonight."

The Wise Woman picks up her teacup, scrutinizes its contents, sips from it thoughtfully. "I'm afraid not tonight," she says, after a pause. "At least not for dinner. I have an . . . an engagement for dinner. I didn't know you'd be getting back last night or . . . ."

"What's up?" I ask. "Who with?"

"It's nothing, really. I should have written you about it, or told you last night. It's nothing serious, of course . . . . But there's this young man. He wants to bring back a couple of my books. I lent them to him months ago." She gestures vaguely. "He lives, rather, lived in the apartment house next door. Last winter when you were away . . . ." She shrugs her shoulders, her hands uplifted. "It's all over. No, that's not right . . . it never really began. I thought about writing you about it, but that's not always the best way, and it wasn't that important anyhow."

"O. K., O. K. Come on, let's hear the whole sordid story."

She smiles. "Well, last winter, we had a snowstorm. A real blizzard. There hadn't been anything like it in years. The Potomac frozen, National shut down, that sort of thing. It was fierce. And beautiful, too."

"Oh?" I ask, dryly.

"Don't be stuffy, dear," she says, but she is smiling. "Do you want me to tell you what happened or don't you?"

"Of course I want you to tell me."

"Well," she gestures towards the living room. "I'd gone to the windows to look out. It had started in mid-afternoon, you know, but I'd been writing and was hardly aware of how much . . . so I went to the living room to see what it was like. And when I got there, I could hear someone singing."

"Singing! In a blizzard?"

She nodded. "And dancing! And playing a saxophone. Imagine! Around a fire. It was beautiful." She shakes her head. "The flames! Incredible. Against the snow — it was still snowing, you know. Snowing hard. I hadn't seen anything like it in years. And this young man and his friend — I forgot to mention it, there were two of them — they were dancing around the fire. And singing. Imagine! Incredible!"

"I'm sure it was," I say, grudgingly. "Fire in the snow . . . . And then what?"

"I simply *couldn't* stay inside. I, well, to make a long story short, I bundled up and went outside. They were really sweet, those boys. They were as high as kites. Like children. Excitement and pleasure," she adds quickly. "No drugs or anything like that. Just high . . . on excitement, and the snow and all that."

"O. K., O. K., so they were high on excitement and the snow."

"It turned out that I knew him. The one who was doing most of the singing. He's an automobile salesman." She ignores my snort. "I bought the VW from him. . . . It turns out they lived in one of the apartments next door. They were like children really. Singing and dancing like a couple of kids." Again she reaches for my hand. "They're much younger than we are, dear; just kids, really . . . . And pretty wonderful, too."

"I'm sure they were," I mutter. "Fire in the snow . . . . Singing and dancing." I wait for her to continue. "And then?"

"Well — now don't laugh, dear — I began dancing too. I felt like a girl again. Almost. It was so beautiful out there! The flames, the shadows against the snow and the trees. It was like a surreal ballet or something of the sort. You'd have loved it."

She smiles. "Well, after the fire had died down, I invited him — the one I'd bought the car from; the other had a date in Georgetown or something — I invited him in for a drink."

"Oh," I say. "I see the scenario shaping up."

"Well, ..." She hesitates. "To make a long story short, he stayed the night."

"Congratulations." I start to get up from the table, but she reaches for my wrist. So I sit down, she pours me some more tea, and then she rises from her chair and kisses me lightly on the forehead.

"You're jealous!" she cries. "Oh, that's wonderful! I'm so glad. . . . Please be jealous."

"Please go on with the story." I make a slight grimace. "Please continue the saga of the singer in the snow and the lady novelist."

"There is no continuation, of course; and stop acting so silly. I never saw him again, except once or twice, when he was taking out the garbage or something like that. He's a child, really." She smiles. "He sent me flowers, a box of candy, even a singing telegram once. I think he wanted me to marry him . . . . it was hard to tell him it was all over. Anyhow, he moved away; I hadn't heard a word from him until a couple of days ago. He wanted to return some books I'd lent him. You could meet him tonight if you want to; we could all have dinner together."

I grimace. "If it weren't for the honor. . . . no, thanks, but no thanks."

"You're really so *awful*," she says, smiling. "You never *did* like to dance, did you?"

———————

THE HATCHET MAN IN THE LIGHTHOUSE

(New Orleans Review; anthologized in
Sudden Fiction: American Short-Short Stories)

THE HATCHET MAN
IN THE LIGHTHOUSE

WE ARE SITTING on the trunk of a fallen palmetto pine, Miss Peaches and I, waiting for the sun to set. Far down the beach, where curving strand and sky meet, we can glimpse the pale blue-pink smudge that is Savannah. Below us, a few vacationers still linger on the sand, but to the east the shore is deserted; it is almost time for us to go home for dinner. The moon has not yet risen; the tide is coming in. Out of nowhere a boy jogs towards us; he is neither city-pale nor tidewater-tan; he looks to be between six and seven years old. A few yards from us he slows down, hesitates, finally stops in front of Miss Peaches.

"Hi," she says, and smiles; so do I.

"Hello," he replies; somewhat formally, a city boy, from Savannah, perhaps, maybe Beaufort. He is a fine-looking youngster, well-built and with clearblue eyes.

"Been swimming?" I ask; a foolish question, his hair is soaking wet. "How was the water?"

"Yes," he says, and scratches in the sand with his toes. "It was very good." Miss Peaches nods agreement. "We've been in twice today. The surf was wonderful. Just right."

The boy starts to say something, hesitates, and points across the shining sea towards the mainland. "I've been *there*, too," he announces. "Have you?"

We nod, the boy squints, and points again. "Do you see *it*?"

"See what?" I ask, squinting in turn.

"The Lighthouse." His voice is mildly patronizing. "Way down there. The Lighthouse."

"There's no lighthouse there," I start to say, but Miss Peaches interrupts.

"Yes," she tells the boy. "We see it."

"Have you ever *been* there?"

"No," I say, "No, we've never been there."

"I have." His voice is firm, it brooks no disagreement. "My Mom and Dad took me there."

"Did they?" Miss Peaches asks. "What fun that must have been. What's the lighthouse like?"

He hesitates. "It's big," he says, after a pause. "It's very big."

He looks through me and beyond me, eyes narrowed, scanning the horizon. "It's big enough for *him*."

"For him?" Miss Peaches and I speak in unison, as though the scene had been rehearsed.

"The hatchet man." His voice is very serious, very earnest. "A giant hatchet man."

"The hatchet man?" I say. "I never knew . . . I mean, what's he like, this hatchet man?"

The boy's clear blue eyes travel from mine, he is seeing something I cannot see.

"He's huge." He gestures with both hands. "He's . . . he's *gargantuan*."

"Is he!" I suppress a smile, shake my head and glance towards Miss Peaches.

The boy nods emphatically. "There are seahorses out there, too." He extends his arms, embracing the entire expanse of land and slowly-darkening sea. "Man-sized seahorses."

"Yes," Miss Peaches says. "We've seen *them*. But we've never seen the hatchet man. What does he *do* there? What's he *like*?"

Again the boy scratches the sand with his toes. "He's very ugly," he says after a long, thoughtful pause. "He's as ugly as *sin*." He hesitates, while I bite my lip to suppress a smile. "But he's very . . . very kind."

"Kind?" I say. "That's good to know. I'm glad to know that he's kind. But why . . . why do you call him the hatchet man?"

He looks at me with diminishing patience. "Because that's who he *is*. Everybody . . . ." He slowly shakes his head as if in disbelief. "*Almost* everybody knows that."

Toward Savannah the blue–pink smudge has turned the color of smoke, but in the east a faint glimmer illuminates the water; soon the moon will be rising, there is a slight offshore breeze but there may be some mosquitoes, it is time for us to go back to the house. I extend my hand toward the boy.

"It's very interesting, all these things. Perhaps we'll see you again tomorrow, and you can tell us more about him. We'd like to hear more about the hatchet man...and the seahorses, too."

He shakes my hand, he no longer seems irritated at my stupidity. "I'll come back," he says. "I'll come back tomorrow morning."

"Be sure to," Miss Peaches says. "We want to hear more about them."

She leans over and runs her hand lightly through his damp hair. He smiles, heads toward the hard-packed sand at the edge of the sea, and turns and waves to us; we wave back.

"My Mom," he calls, his voice clear and distinct. "My Mom's dead."

We say nothing as he turns again and jogs off, well-coordinated, light on his feet, he will become a good middle-distance runner. Miss Peaches and I watch him, without speaking, until he is only a speck in the distance. I think he stops once again to wave, but at that distance and without my glasses I cannot be sure.

———————

ELLEN'S GIFT

(Texas Review)

ELLEN'S GIFT

BEFORE ELLEN DIED, we talked a lot about her last semester at the University. It had been good, she said, very good indeed. For a while everything had seemed to fall into place that semester, her writing, her teaching her first classes, even her troubled marriage. And no, she said, speaking quietly and unemotionally as though referring to someone she had known only slightly; no, she really *wasn't* afraid any more; she had somehow put aside all those fears when the doctors had told her after her last operation that she was terminal.

"It's strange," she said, "but that doesn't worry me any more, it really doesn't." She paused, half-closing her eyes. "I had not known how many friends I have. I never had many friends before, you know. I have been lucky, really."

And then, suddenly, she had started to cry, and she clumsily pulled the blanket over her head like a child discovered in the act of doing something naughty; and after a minute or two I tiptoed out of the room and quietly, very quietly, closed the door behind me.

She never *had* had many friends; Ellen's gifts were of the mind, not the body. She was the most talented student I had ever known, a Southwestern Flannery O'Connor who spoke with her own voice, saw people and incidents through her own process of vision: her stories, even from the first, were without a false move or an unnecessary detail, and as uncompromisingly real as the cancer that was killing her before her career had begun.

"You must stay only a few minutes," the nurse admonished me a few days later. She shook her head slowly and glanced towards the closed door of Ellen's room.

"She has been very tired."

I nodded. I had talked with the doctor earlier that afternoon. "No way," he had said; "a week maybe; who can say?"

"She has been asking to see you," the nurse whispered as she opened the door.

"She has been asking all afternoon when you were coming."

Again I nodded, and entered the room. Ellen lay on her back, the light blanket accentuating rather than concealing the swell of her abdomen. She smiled when she saw me, but she did not speak. I sat down by her bedside, and reached for her hand. For a long time I sat there, holding her hand, while the pinkness slowly faded from the sky until, beyond her window, the lights from the College across the drive were twinkling like fireflies. We did not talk. I just sat there and I could not tell if she were asleep or awake until suddenly she withdrew her hand.

With difficulty she fumbled for the call button at the side of her bed, but the effort was too much and she lay back, breathing heavily, and pointed toward the button. I pushed it, and we sat there without speaking until the nurse came into the room. Ellen pointed toward the blanket-covered swell of her body; her lips framed the words *help me*.

"Go out for a minute, please," the nurse said in a low voice. "She . . . she has something to show you."

Her voice trailed away, so I tiptoed out of the room. I waited for what seemed a long time. And then the door opened, and the nurse was standing in front of me. She has talked about this with the doctor, she said, almost disapprovingly, and then she lowered her voice and whispered something I could not understand, and I followed her into the room. Ellen seemed more asleep than awake. The scar extended from her navel to her pelvis. It was neither unpleasant nor disfiguring; paradoxically, there was something about it not undesirable, a wound stripe, clean and antiseptic; the flesh around the sutured edges almost as translucent in the fading light as the skin of a fish.

I stood there for a long moment. I did not look at Ellen, but I think she was smiling ever so slightly before the nurse lowered the gown over her wounded body and replaced the light blanket.

"It is almost time for supper," she said, and left the room, quietly closing the door behind her.

I sat there in the gathering darkness, holding Ellen's hand, and waited for the attendant to arrive.

———————

FAMILY PORTRAIT

(Carleton Miscellany)

FAMILY PORTRAIT

I

MY FATHER DIED OF A STROKE at the age of sixty. Weeding in his flower garden. I found him lying there a few minutes after breakfast, a small spading fork and a trowel by his side; the peatmoss in the trowel was still cool and moist. His blue eyes were open and I think he recognized me but he could neither speak nor move. I took off my jacket and placed it carefully over his shoulders.

"I'll be right back, Dad, don't worry, don't try to move."

I run to the house (it is a Wednesday, my mother left shortly after breakfast to do the week's groceries). I call our family doctor and hurry back to the garden. My father lies dead among the dahlias he never got to show at the county fair.

He had not been a great success. Worked in the local bank most of his life. After a quarter of a century became vice president, but that is as far as he ever went.

My mother wanted him to be president of the bank and mayor of the town. A quiet, gentle man whom I never really knew. Had few close friends.

Neither drank nor smoked.

From a family of small farmers (landowners, my mother said), shopkeepers (business men, my mother said), school teachers, an occasional doctor or lawyer, ministers, and religious fanatics.

Seldom if ever cursed. Only once do I remember hearing him curse.

It was after dinner, one summer night. I was eight or nine. My father had been puttering around in the basement where he had a workshop of a sort (with gardening, his only hobby). My mother had been pestering him to do some kind of chore in the kitchen, repairing a leak in the icebox or fixing a light or something. Kept calling him to come up from the basement, which he finally did. Grudgingly. Rummaged around beneath the sink where he'd left a heavy wrench or something. Straightened up too soon. Banged his head terribly, knocked off his glasses, crushed them with his feet or with the wrench, I could hear the lenses tinkling, he was terribly near-sighted.

"Damn," he said, not loud but deep. On his hands and knees, fumbling for the broken lenses, rubbing his bruised forehead.

"Damn! God Almighty, JESUS CHRIST!"

"Walter! How could you!" Mother's back straight as an arrow. Transfixed him with a glance.

"Damn," he said again, trying to straighten out the bent frame. For a terrible minute I thought he was going to cry; never in my entire life, not once, had I ever seen my father cry.

"GODALMIGHTYJESUSCHRISTGODDAMN!"

Mother went to her room, closed the door, stayed there for a week.

I never heard him curse again, not ever.

II

I never knew my father well. He gave me more than I ever gave him. He made things grow.

A few weeks before my eleventh birthday, I was haunted.

Maniacs in the next county had predicted that the world was coming to an end. Precisely at midnight, they said, at a specified date in late September. Sold all their belongings and took refuge on a nearby hill, hardly even a hill, this was tidewater country. Waiting to be saved, all others would be damned. I was terrified.

Fear and dread my constant companions.

Dared not speak about it to anybody.

I joined the Episcopal Church — my father was an ordained deacon — before my birthday. Tried to discuss the end of the world with the minister. Could not.

That last night before the end of the world was awful. I lay in bed, staring at the ceiling, waiting for the heavens to split apart. Finally tiptoed down the long dark hall to my parents' bedroom. The door was ajar, but I knocked as I'd been taught to.

My father and mother were sitting by the opened windows. It was hot for late September, but they'd turned off the lights against the mosquitos. From the bedside the lemony odor of a citronella candle. Patches of fog, and from the bay the recurring *blaat* of a foghorn.

"Yes?" my mother said, without turning from the window.

Courage, resolve, left me, I mumbled something, and retreated to my room.

A few minutes later, I heard my father's knock at my door. He didn't speak. Just pulled a chair close to my bed. Scratched my back. "You're feverish, son," he said. Sat there beside me in silence. Put his hand on mine. Said nothing, just sat there in the darkness, his hand resting lightly on my own, listening to the sound of the foghorn and looking out into the dark yard and the tall wildcherry trees beyond the kitchen garden.

A dam in me broke. "Is the world really going to come to an end tonight?" I told him everything.

"No," he said, finally. "The world's not going to come to an end tonight." Patted my hand. "The world's always coming to an end, son. For somebody. But not for us, not tonight. Not for us." He ran his hands lightly through my hair. "You need a haircut, son. We'll go to the barber's tomorrow morning."

Squeezed my hand, started to say something else, but tiptoed away in silence.

A taciturn man, not given to demonstrations.

––––––

ACROSS THE HALL

(New Orleans Review)

ACROSS THE HALL

THE FLIGHT HAD BEEN BUMPY all the way to New Orleans, and Jackson breathed a long sigh of relief when the plane finally touched down at the New Orleans airport. "I don't like flying," he muttered, as much to himself as to Helen, his wife. "Let's face it, I just *don't* like it." But by the time they had checked into their hotel in the center of the French Quarter and they had taken a short rest and showered he was more than ready for some drinks and a good meal at Galatoire's or the Court of the Two Sisters. The ice machine was at the far end of the long, carpeted corridor, and Jackson wasn't aware of the footsteps behind him as he filled his ice bucket and, turning, spilled some of the cubes on the tasseled tan loafers of the man behind him.

"Sorry," he mumbled, terribly embarrassed, and quickly bent over to brush away the offending ice. "I . . . ."

"No matter," the man replied quickly. His voice was as pleasant as his ruddy face, unlined and crowned with a broad forehead and a mane of magnificent snow-white hair. "Weren't we on the same plane? Out of Miami? Flight 903?"

"Yes," Jackson said. "And I'm mighty glad it's over. One of the roughest flights I can remember."

The man nodded. "You can say that again!"

Jackson refilled the ice bucket, nodded, and hurried down the long corridor. He set the ice bucket down, carefully, and with some difficulty opened the door. He gasped: a young woman was sitting on the king-sized bed, her face half-buried in her hands. At the sound, she looked up, startled. She was young, beautiful, and as naked as a jaybird. The tips of her small breasts were rouged, and on her face was a look of unutterable grief, as devastating as the St. Gaudens statue of the suicide wife of Henry Adams.

He instinctively closed his eyes, flushing from his violation of the naked young woman's privacy, and hurried across the hall; Helen was doing things to her hair, beautiful, waist-length, and as smooth as silk.

"What kept you?" she began, turned, and then rose swiftly. "What's the matter, dear? You look as though you'd just seen a ghost."

"Nothing," he said. "Uh, nothing at all." Carefully, he placed the ice bucket on the desk near the window, fumbled in his tote bag, and withdrew the oblong bottle of Jack Daniel's. Helen was looking at him quizzically; she raised her index finger and, smiling, shook it at him reprovingly.

"Don't try to fool *me*, dear; what's the matter?"

"Nothing," he repeated, and carefully poured the whiskey. He turned to hand Helen her drink. From across the hall a terrible cry shattered the quiet; the glass slipped from his fingers.

"Good Lord!" Helen cried. "What was that?"

Across the hall, a door slammed, hard.

———————

THE BLUE SLIPPER

(Writers' Forum)

THE BLUE SLIPPER

I

IN THE DREAM I am a painter, smeared smock, beret, battered paint box and all. I have set up my easel, rather insecurely, on a grassy slope overlooking a river. The place seems unfamiliar at first, but as I remove my brushes and tubes of paint, it becomes vaguely recognizable. Very much like Goshen Pass, but the river beneath me is less turbulent than it was years ago when it was called simply North River and roared whitely over jagged rocks (when I was young I could dive from those rocks where misjudging the swiftness of the current or the location of the deep pools could mean a broken neck).

It is a happy moment. I find myself humming snatches of a long-forgotten song — *bell bottom trousers coat of navy blue* — but without warning my euphoria vanishes. The sky darkens, a cold wind whistles through the pine trees, my eyes are drawn to something in the river, and the skin at the base of my skull tightens in apprehension. Floating downstream (at least fifty yards away but I see them clearly and distinctly) floating as sedately as a lily pad in a quiet pond.

A pair of small bedroom slippers!

They are decorated with cat-and-dog-and-mouse figures labelled policeman, nurse, fireman, postman, doctor, aviator. Now they are floating directly beneath me, and suddenly the black sky closes in upon me. I wake up, drenched with sweat, trembling in terror.

II

At breakfast, somewhere between the orange juice and the granola, I tell Margaret about the dream (she is in the psychology department; her major interest is the sub-conscious).

"What do you make of that one?" I ask.

"I'm not sure. It's interesting, but not unusual. Not terribly unusual, that is." She ponders a moment or two, shrugs her shoulders. "It's about loss, I think. Loss of some kind, that seems clear enough. You said there were animals on the slippers? Cats and dogs?"

"That's right, cats and dogs. But they were dressed up. In children's costumes. And they were labelled." I close my eyes, trying to reconstruct the scene on the river. "They were standing on something, each of them.

I can't recall exactly. Maybe small platforms or something of the sort. And they were labelled, very clearly and distinctly: n-u-r-s-e or f-i-r-e-m-a-n or d-o-c-t-o-r or p-o-l-i-c-e-m-a-n or whatever. Very clearly. I could see the words as clearly as I can see you now."

"I'll have to think about that," she says. "It's very interesting. That part particularly."

"You're not much help," I say, smiling. "How about you? Did you dream anything?"

"Not much." She half-closes her eyes and rubs her forehead. "I did dream something, but it's faded away. Nothing like that dream of yours. Let me think about it for a while."

III

A few days later, after breakfast, we go upstairs to our studies. I hardly have time to remove the cover from the typewriter when I hear Margaret hurrying down the long hall (we have separate studies at opposite ends of our old house) and she bursts into my room, which is a violation of our number-one house rule not to disturb each other on the rare mornings when each of us can stay at home and try to catch up on our own writing or research.

"Joe!" she cries. "Look what I just found!"

She holds aloft a small blue bedroom slipper and carefully places it on my desk next to my typewriter. It is made of corduroy and has a slightly-worn blue rubber sole; it is zippered and decorated with tiny figures of cats and dogs labelled *nurse, fireman, doctor, policeman,* and so on.

"I'll be damned," I say, after a long pause. I stroke the slipper absent-mindedly, the corduroy is surprisingly firm, had I expected to find it limp and damp with river water? Carefully I return it to my typewriter table.

"Where in the world did you find *that*?"

"It was on the couch. In my study." She shakes her head slowly.

"On your *couch*?"

She nods.

"You haven't suddenly gone bonkers, have you? It's...."

"I know," she interrupts. "It's exactly like the one in your dream."

"Incredible!" I pick it up and examine it: sixteen tiny figures, kittens and puppies dressed like firemen, nurses, policemen. "This is hard to believe. What do you think?"

"I don't know what to think. It really gave me a turn, suddenly seeing it there on the couch."

"Could one of the grand-children have left it here?"

She shakes her head vigorously. "I thought of that, the first thing. But it couldn't have been; they were here the weekend *before* you had the dream, remember? And besides, Ardella would have found it the day after they left, when she cleaned; she's always on the lookout for artifacts after they've been here. She's cleaned the study half a dozen times since then."

"Yes," I say, grudgingly. "It couldn't have been one of the kids."

Margaret leans over, picks up the slipper, scrutinizes it in silence. "Besides, this is a much older slipper than the kind they make nowadays." She puts on the reading glasses suspended by a black ribbon around her neck. "I had a pair of slippers like this once.... They haven't made slippers like this for years."

"Then what? How in the world did it...?"

"I don't know. I honestly have no idea."

"Perhaps it could have been our poltergeist?"

"Don't be silly."

"Why don't you call up Susan? Ask *her* if either of the kids left one of their slippers here."

She tries to put her hand into the slipper. "Rick or Billy couldn't get their foot into this slipper. This is an infant's slipper, not a child's."

She passes it to me, with some difficulty I unzip it. I can hardly get the tips of my fingers into it.

"You're right. It *is* too small. What next?"

"Lord, I don't know." She looks at her watch. "I've got to get back to work. There's a rational explanation for all this, of course. Let me think about it."

She goes back to her study; in a minute or two I hear the typewriter clicking away. I sit quietly, holding the slipper in my hand.

IV

After lunch, Margaret leaves for the university. I go back to my study. The blue slipper is on the typewriter table where I had left it. I pretend to work, riffling through my notes for an article I am supposed to do for one of the quarterlies, but my mind wanders so I decide to meditate (we have been meditators for three years and though I view with some skepticism their current reports of levitation, we both agree that we've benefitted a lot from meditating...who knows, really?). Usually we meditate fifteen or twenty minutes before breakfast and then again before dinner, but occasionally, when I'm home in the afternoon, I try to work in another session by myself. I am a pragmatist in most ways, but I do believe in ESP, TM, the power of the mind over the body, and things like that. And then a couple of years ago there was all that business about the poltergeist in our kitchen....

So I pull down the shade and compose myself, my breathing slows, my heartbeat moderates, words float into my consciousness along with my mantra: *footfalls echo in the memory/down the passage which we did not take/toward the door we never opened....* And then I hear it, a child's voice:

daddy

from far away:

daddy

it sounds as though somehow it is floating out of the fireplace in the corner of my study:

daddy daddy daddy

followed by scarcely audible weeping, cries so faint as to be beyond belief but alive with almost unbearable anguish....

Slowly I come back to the world, open my eyes, scan the comfortable study with all the things I know and love: my books, hundreds and hundreds of them, the pictures, the record player, the walnut liquor cabinet, the framed graduation photographs of our children, the snapshots of our grandchildren....

I am back in the world but I was not imagining those cries. I heard them, the cries of the child who was never born. I heard them but I think I shall not tell Margaret about them. Later, yes, but not today.

———————

HUSBAND AND WIFE

(Roanoke Review)

HUSBAND AND WIFE

ALL DAY, EVERY DAY, Jasper's wife Anna kept worrying him, walking around the apartment with tears in her beautiful gray eyes. "You used to say," she would whisper, "you used to say you couldn't have enough of me. You used to tell me you loved me, every morning. You would never walk by me without reaching out and touching me. Now you ignore me. You never cuddle me, never let me sit on your lap any more. Why don't you cuddle me; why don't you let me sit on your lap any more?"

"I do love you, honey babe," Jasper would say, looking up from the littered desk where he sat the mornings away, listlessly gazing out of the window or rising nervously to limp around the book-lined study, trying to get a story started, though it had been months – or was it years? – since he had really completed a piece of fiction. "I do love you, but it is an imperfect world, dear heart, and all human relationships are imperfect, too." He would sigh, and remove his steel-rimmed glasses, the sole remnant of his three years in the Army, and gingerly stretch out his legs, flexing and unflexing his toes within the wornout tennis shoes. "It is an imperfect world," he would repeat, more to himself than to Anna, and gaze sadly at the blank page in the typewriter on the table beside the great desk, "a very imperfect world."

So he would sit, morning after long morning, occasionally removing his aching legs from a flowered ottoman and rising to call to Anna that he still loved her or to limp around the study, stopping to look at the faded backs of the magazines where his stories had been published. Alas, how few there were, *Accent, Story, discovery*,. . . . Almost every magazine he published in had subsequently expired, and he sometimes, whimsically yet with an uncomfortable feeling of truth, felt that he was a Jonah, that he was without talent or even ability, that his stories were in effect the kiss of death.

"This is very little to show for ten years of hard work, honey babe," he called out one particularly unproductive morning when his legs felt as though they were made of chalk and would snap beneath his weight at any moment. It had rained all during the night, quietly and persistently, and the winter landscape was as gray as a mouse. He had slept badly, slowly turning and writhing throughout his long night, and by morning his arthritis had so stiffened his hands that he could hardly make a fist. Now he sat and looked out upon the dismal world beyond his window where a single bedraggled sparrow shivered on the gutter of the sloping roof. His bones ached and he rose with difficulty to walk slowly around the room, tentatively rising and descending on his toes to restore his circulation.

"This is very little to be proud of, dear babe," he called again, waving his hands in the general direction of the magazines, "very little to be proud of."

"What's that, lover?" Anna called from the bedroom where she was sewing. "Did you call me?"

"I said," Jasper repeated, "that I have very little to be proud of."

"Oh, dear," she said.

He could hear her getting to her feet. Something metallic, a pair of scissors perhaps, clattered to the bedroom floor, and then she was standing in the doorway of the study, a gentle, fair-haired woman in her late thirties. "What is it, lover, what is it?"

He half rose from his chair and gazed upon her sadly. "You know, dear babe, I feel as though my legs were made of chalk." He shook his shoulders, flexed and unflexed his hands. "My arthritis is simply crippling me. I'll be a cripple some time, you know, a goddamned cripple."

"Oh no," she cried, crossing the room swiftly and placing her hand on his shoulder. "Oh, Jasper, you mustn't say that. It's not true, lover, simply not true. You're in wonderful shape for . . . ."

"For what? For a man my age? For a man who will be forty next month? Nyahh," he groaned, but with a faint, sad smile in his eyes. "I'm falling apart, dear babe, that's what I'm doing, falling apart."

She bent over and kissed him, breathing warmly into his ear. "You're not falling apart, lover," she said, and sat on his lap in one swift, graceful movement. He shifted uneasily as she settled into the once-comfortable position, and averted his eyes.

"Don't pull away, lover," she said, "please don't pull away."

"I'm not pulling away, dear babe," he said, but again shifted uneasily beneath her weight. "But you'll have to get up, honey babe; my legs feel as if they were breaking. Honest to God, they feel as though they were breaking."

She rose slowly and stood beside him. "You don't love me any more. Why don't you love me any more?"

"Not true," he said. "Simply not true." Painfully he extended his legs, curling and uncurling his toes and rubbing his legs. "It's simply not true, dear babe, but let's face it. I'm too damned weak to hold you on my lap any more." He leaned over and removed his tennis shoes and again rested his legs on the ottoman. "Ah, that's good," he muttered, closing his eyes in contentment, gently massaging his calves. "That's very good, dear babe." When she did not answer he opened his eyes and stared at the empty doorway. "Anna," he called. "Anna, darling. Where are you, honey babe?"

At the sound of her sobs, he started to rise from his chair. Then half in resignation, half in pique, he lay back and continued to flex and unflex his toes. "Anna," he called again, "come on back, honey babe."

Again she was in the doorway, gazing at him uncertainly.

"Come in, honey babe," he repeated. "I feel fine now. Come sit down."

She entered hesitantly, and he extended his arms.

"Oh, lover," she cried. She stroked his shoulders with her strong fingers.

"Don't work for a while," she said. "Stop working, dear heart."

Gently she eased herself into his lap. Jasper shifted slightly, and gave a sudden, high scream. His legs snapped like pieces of chalk as he fell to the floor; all he could see was Anna's face, a face transformed into an unrecognizable mask.

———————

CYCLOPS

(Open Places)

CYCLOPS

SUNDAY AFTERNOON in San Francisco. Half of Union Square Plaza in the shade, the other half-bathed in almost Mediterranean sunlight. I see an empty bench, and we hurry to it. I take off my jacket, stretch my legs, loosen my tie. How good the sun feels on a face ashen from six weeks of pre-Winter Missouri weather. We like Missouri, although every autumn we wonder why we have stayed there all these years. True, we have a good department, and both Miss Peaches and I love our old house: many rooms, high ceilings, lots of space for our books and pictures. But the weather! And the mouse-colored winter landscape, low skies, damp as a Gothic graveyard, chilling the spirit and numbing the body . . . .

I reach for Miss Peaches' hand. "I'm glad we decided not to go to that seminar."

She nods, I rub my bad knee, squint through half-closed eyes at the glorious sun. Beyond the palmetto-dotted plaza, people are streaming through the doors of Macy's for the post-Christmas sales; to our left towers the high facades of the hotel where we are staying during the annual meetings; behind us three or four black men lay sprawled on the warm grass.

I am pleasantly high, more from the sun than the vodka martinis we had with lunch. It is like being at a zoo: such a host parading before us, a circus: a beautiful young woman in a see-through blouse, her breasts an army with banners, pushing an expensive baby carriage in which one black child and one white child sit as erect as statues; a gigantic American Indian in a pink suit and white leghorn hat from which bright ostrich plumes tumble upon his shoulder-length hair; a paraplegic on a wheeled platform drawn by a magnificent Saint Bernard; a lean cattleman in high-heeled boots (as he passes I catch a pungent whiff of marijuana).

Gradually, separate voices emerge from the collective hum, and from them specific words and phrases. One voice in particular floats to the surface, soft, slurred, but as distinct as the *Amen* in the Episcopal communion service.

Bleep

I am slightly offended. I dislike the word primarily because it has become a commonplace in the vocabulary of so many of my students.

Bleep

Low, but penetrating, followed by a pause, an intake of breath as though the speaker had just completed a marathon, praying for oxygen. Soft, wise, ancient as the hills. By now I am alert, listening; the voice is from one of the men sprawled on the grassy slope behind us.

Charlottesville.

I am really alert now. I used to live there.

Vinegar Hill . . . . . Bleep.

I listen carefully but the voice is momentarily blotted out by a passing plane.

I shall never know what happened on Vinegar Hill.

Bill Cosby, the voice is saying. Could trust him . . . all the way . . . sewed up my pockets 'fore I'd step onto those streets . . . forty geeks . . . make a thousand a week in Vegas . . . BLEEP! Mama Cass . . . My eye? The pigs did that.

People pass before us: the prototype English professor from out of town, his ill-fitting tweed far too heavy for this sunny afternoon; a fat man in Bermuda shorts carrying a fox-terrier in a wicker basket; another Texan, younger and paler than the pot- smoker (there's a warrant out for me in Bernalillo county, he is telling his prostitute companion) . . . .

Behind us, the slow, slurred voice has never ceased, unhurried, unruffled, seldom more than a few words at a time and then a pause, the slow intake of breath, followed by the once-forbidden verb, a caesura, a prayer, a call to arms, a last hurrah . . . .

He has been everywhere, the owner of that voice: freaked out with Teddy at Chappaquiddick, almost drowned in the Tidal Basin with Fanny Fox, underwent psychiatric treatment with James Earl Ray in the Springfield pen, lasted half a round with Muhammad Ali, sang with Sinatra, boogered Zsa Zsa Gabor, expelled from Hampton Institute for peddling grass, Purple Heart for service in Vietnam, was rolled on 42nd Street, tamped out a cigarette in W. Gordon Liddy's navel . . . .

A flicker of coolness along my spine; we are no longer in the sun. I lean towards Miss Peaches. "I hate to leave that." I lower my voice, resisting the temptation to turn, to discover the identity of the speaker. "But weren't we supposed to meet someone?"

"I'm afraid so," she says.

I stretch my legs; my knee, warmed by the sun, feels pretty good. I put on my jacket, turn around; the shock almost takes my breath away: he is huge, very black, bald as an apple, and one-eyed: Cyclops, Sinbad, Homer, Ancient Mariner, a Magus. I look straight into his good eye, hoping, soliciting, begging, almost demanding recognition. But the old artificer refuses the gambit. He is above and beyond me or Miss Peaches: Olympian, aloof, godlike. I look at the soothsayer one last time; his eye stares through me as if I were a pane of glass. We step to the sidewalk; I hear the magic word for the last time:

Bleep, says the old artificer: *bleep, bleep, bleep.*

BOONE COUNTY PARABLE

(Boone County Fare; anthologized,
Norton Anthology of Short Fiction, 2nd ed., 1981)

BOONE COUNTY PARABLE

WE RODE OUR BIKES to the shopping center that afternoon. Usually in mid-July it's too hot in Little Dixie to ride, but this was like October in the Shenandoah Valley. Miss Peaches wanted to buy some dress material and I waited outside the fabric store with the bikes. Four-thirty, and the shopping center was almost empty. Then a man was approaching me, a countryman, about thirty, with a curiously blank, unlined, pleasant face; he had very dark hair and he wore a clean t-shirt and stained tan work-pants and he was unbelievably cross-eyed. As he came near me, I stepped back from the edge of the sidewalk, our faces met, I nodded.

"Hi," I said.

He hesitated. "Hello," he said.

"Beautiful afternoon," I said. "Beautiful."

He stopped and looked at me — that is, his crossed eyes revolved towards me — and he smiled a very tentative smile, and when I smiled back he extended his hand.

"Yes," he said. "Beautiful."

We shook hands.

"I went fishing last night," he said abruptly. His voice was flat, pleasant, a slight drawl, slightly nasal, a good Little Dixie voice.

"Did you?" I asked. "Any luck?"

He smiled, no longer tentatively, and again his crossed eyes revolved towards me. "Caught two flatheads. Big ones."

"Good," I said. "Whereabouts?"

"On Perchee Crick." He half-closed his eyes, ran his hands through his hair.

"Got caught too."

"Caught?" I asked. "What do you mean, caught? Didn't you have a fishing license?"

He pointed towards his hip pocket. "Game warden caught me. But I had my license all the time. In my wallet."

"Ah, good," I said.

Beyond the Drive-In Theater we heard the whinney of a horse, a high, imperious laughing. The man shook his head slowly before confronting me with his crossed eyes.

"That's not all," he said. "There was an accident at the crick."

"Oh?" I asked. "I hadn't heard....I haven't seen the paper today."

"From the bridge," he said. "Someone fell on the rocks from the bridge."

"From the bridge? Is that right?"

"My daughter," he said. "It was my daughter that fell from the bridge."

"Good Lord," I said. "I hope...."

He interrupted me with a wave of his hand, the crossed eyes circled around and beyond me, the strangely-sweet empty face was unchanged.

"She didn't last very long," he said.

"I'm sorry," I stammered, "I..." but he raised his hand, palm-up, the stained fingers outspread.

"She didn't last hardly at all."

"I'm sorry," I said again, "I...."

"Thanks," he said, friendship and recognition in his voice and unlined face. His voice was hardly audible, and then he turned and I watched him until he disappeared into the dime store.

Miss Peaches came out with the material a few minutes later, and I fastened the package in the clamp over my rear mudguard.

"There'll be a lot of traffic from the M.F.A.," I said. "Be careful."

We rode our bikes across the almost-empty parking lot, down the winding road alongside the Drive-In, and past the Fair Grounds and the show ring where a couple of pre-teenagers were trotting their ponies. A steady stream of cars from the M.F.A. Insurance Office inched down Ash

Street, and I eased very carefully onto the road, looked back at Miss Peaches, keeping as close to the curb as possible. A pale green Cadillac crept up behind me, then along-side me, crowding me. I looked at the driver behind the tightly-closed windows, pale, redhaired, thirtyish doughface, and I gestured towards her to move over, to give me room, but she kept crowding me till my ankle scraped painfully against the curb, my bike wobbled for a moment, then my foot was on the curb, the bike was steady, and the red-headed woman and the Cadillac moved on.

"Are you all right?" Miss Peaches was calling behind me. "Are you all right?"

"Yes," I said. "I'm all right." I pointed towards the receding pale green car. I could scarcely see the woman's redhead above the steering wheel. "Goddamned mother," I said. "Goddamned lowborn mother."

———————

BELOW FREEZING

(Texas Review)

BELOW FREEZING

WHEN I WAS A BOY my mother always opened the windows at night no matter what the weather. Winters then were seldom very cold; we lived near tidewater, at dusk the air stirred with the smell of salt and clean living things. But sometimes there would be a hard freeze and my mother would put a heavy comforter at the foot of my bed when she came to my room to see if I was still awake.

For Heaven's sake, she would say, please go to sleep, and don't forget to say your prayers, and she would walk slowly from the room without touching me, making sure to check the window before she closed the door.

I would lie quietly and listen to the sound of her footsteps receding down the long hall and when I heard her door close I would steal out of my bed — how cold the floor to my bare feet — and tiptoe to the window and search the sky behind the bare limbs of the wild cherry trees.

Sometimes I could see or I thought I could see the pale pink dot that was Mars and then I would think of John Carter of Virginia and like him I would stretch out my arms towards the pale glow and close my eyes half-wishing half-fearing that like John Carter of Virginia I would be whirled senseless through time and space and wake up on the pink star with Thuvia the Maid of Mars and the Warlords of Mars and the eight-legged mammoths whose name I can no longer remember.

I would stand there by the window for a long time before crawling back into my narrow bed, more dead than alive from cold and grief, forget to say my prayers, and fall asleep.

Sometimes in the early morning there would be a skim of ice on the surface of the goldfish bowl on top of my bookcase, as thin as the skin of an egg. I would poke my finger through it and wait for the cold nibbling kiss from the people in the fishbowl.

Now the windows are all sealed, the air is heavy with the smell of garbage and sulphur, and on these inland nights the pale pink planet no longer beckons from beyond the frozen trees. The Vikings have landed, Thuvia and John Carter and the Warlords are dead, the cold gnaws at my bones as the old house creaks and the dry timbers shrink. I lie in a new cold bed, half-wishing half- fearing that the furnace in the basement will blow up.

But in the morning, particularly if the sun is shining, I am very glad that it didn't.

———————

MAIN CURRENTS IN AMERICAN THOUGHT

(*Chariton Review*)

MAIN CURRENTS
IN AMERICAN THOUGHT

OUR LAST NIGHT in San Francisco and we were packing our luggage when the phone rang.

"It's Eleanor," Miss Peaches announced.

"Ah," I said, without much enthusiasm. My sister and I hadn't seen much of each other in recent years; she and her first husband had left Washington about the same time Miss Peaches and I had, they to California, we to Missouri. We'd never been very fond of each other, particularly when we were children, but in recent years we'd been exchanging presents at Christmas, sending each other birthday cards, and things like that.

"I'm so sorry I wasn't able to go to Sausalito with you and Peaches this afternoon," she was saying. "But I had one of my headaches. Did you have a good time?"

"Yes," I said. "We're sorry, too. Next time we're in San Francisco . . . ."

"But it's been years since you and Peaches were in San Francisco."

"I know, Eleanor. I'm really sorry. I wish we could see more of each other."

"Oh, so do I. I do wish we could. I'm very proud of you, Bob." Eleanor's voice was affectionate and I began to suspect a trap.

"Proud? Of me?" I glanced at Miss Peaches and made a revolving movement with my index finger above my forehead. "Um, well, uh...I mean that's very nice of you, Eleanor. I appreciate that. But...."

"I was in Gump's a few days ago and your new novel was all over the place. There was a picture of you, and everything. I was so proud."

"My *only* novel," I corrected. "My first and probably last."

"Oh? Why? I thought you'd done other novels. Maybe I was thinking about your short stories. And all those other books, the dry ones . . . . I really do like *Dusk on Monument Avenue*, though. It was good of you to send it to me for Christmas. I was proud."

"It's not that much, Eleanor. It hasn't broken any sales records, you know."

"Oh, that's too bad. But they had a lot of them at Gump's. I was so proud."

"That's very nice of you, Eleanor." I shook my head slowly and looked at Miss Peaches who had resumed packing our luggage. "Sometimes I wish it had never been published, though. I've . . . ."

"Never been published? Why?"

"The book didn't go over too big in Washington, Eleanor. I've lost a few friends there, I'm afraid."

"Oh, that's too bad. But, Bob," Eleanor lowered her voice. "I'm not really surprised, in a way, that is. I mean, it's a pretty vulgar book."

"*Vulgar*? What do you mean, vulgar?"

"Cousin Hugh sent me a review from one of the papers. I can't remember which; maybe it was the *Washington Post*. Yes, that's what it was, the *Post*. They called it . . . uh . . . I think they called it scabrous. Yes, that's what they said, scabrous. Did you see that review?"

"No," I lied. "I never read reviews."

"Cousin Hugh was really upset."

"Cousin Hugh was upset? Why?"

"He said he thought the book was . . . ." Eleanor hesitated. "He thought it was — uh — dirty. He said he thought the scene with the professor and the librarian — you know, the scene after the party — he said that part was obscene."

"Oh, for Pete's sake, Eleanor."

"And he said he thought the professor sounded exactly like you. Tell me, Bob," again she lowered her voice, "are those people there really like *that*? Like that dean? And the librarian? That scene when. . . ."

"Eleanor, I've told you before that I've never written about real people, I mean people I actually knew."

"Oh, Bob, some of them sound exactly like you. Or some of those friends of yours . . . ."

"I've told you before, Eleanor . . . ."

"You knew how furious Cousin Hugh was about one of your stories, didn't you?"

"No, I didn't know. What story?"

"I thought I'd written you about that."

"No, damn it, you never . . . . *What* story?"

"I can't remember the name," she said, "But Cousin Hugh was furious."

"*Furious*? Why was the old bastard furious?"

Miss Peaches closed one of the suitcases and placed a remonstrative hand on my arm. "Stop cursing," she whispered sternly, but she was smiling.

"What's Peaches saying?" Eleanor asked.

"She's telling me to stop cursing."

"You really should try to, you know. It always upset Mother when you swore. Do you remember that time at Virginia Beach when . . . ?"

"Why was Cousin Hugh furious?"

"He was angry because of something you wrote about Mother"

"I never wrote anything about Mother. She was never in any story of mine. He was out of his tree if he said that!"

"And he said," Eleanor paused. "He said he was sick and tired of all that talk about breasts in your novel. He said . . . ."

"Breasts? What does he mean, all that talk about breasts?"

"Oh, Bob! That character, the dean's wife; you're always mentioning her breasts."

"You're insane, Eleanor, absolutely insane. And Cousin Hugh, he's sick. They'll have to put that old goat to sleep one of these days."

"He said you were obsessed — that was his word, Bob — *obsessed*. And he said Mother had been terribly worried about you. When you were a boy. He said . . . ."

"Oh, for the love of Heaven, Eleanor!"

"Mother *was* worried about you, Bob. I remember. Terribly worried. She . . . ."

"Oh, come off it!"

"Don't you remember? When she found those pictures you and Johnny Kellett had drawn?"

"What pictures?"

"The ones Mother found. You and Johnny had drawn them. They were hidden in your bookcase."

"Madness. Absolute madness! That was forty years ago, Eleanor. Almost half a century! Mother had a memory like an elephant, Eleanor. And so do you."

"You're not that old, Bob. It can't be forty years ago."

"Oh, come off it, Eleanor." I glanced at Miss Peaches who had raised a cautioning finger, but it seemed that her lips were framing the words *What pictures?*

"You're angry, aren't you, Bob?" my sister was saying. "I didn't mean to. . . ."

"Of course I'm not angry."

"Are you sure you're not angry?"

"Look, Eleanor, I'm *not* angry. And I *will* try to stop cursing. But we have an early flight tomorrow, and it's time to go to dinner."

"You're sure you're not angry?"

"For the love of Heaven, Eleanor."

"And I really did like your novel. It's just as funny as it can be."

"That's very nice, Eleanor."

"Some of those scenes really broke me up. But, Bob, may I say something?"

"Of course, Eleanor; haven't you always?"

"Are you sure you won't be angry?"

"Of course, I'm sure."

"Well, you know I love the book. I really do, but there's a . . . ." She hesitated; I could imagine her studying her overlong, highly-polished fingernails.

"There's a *what*? For the love of Heaven, Eleanor, *what*?"

"I hesitate to say this, Bob." She paused, laughing lightly in a con-sciously self-deprecating fashion. "I thought you should know, Bob. There's a grammatical error. . . on page ninety. I thought. . . ."

———

ENDANGERED SPECIES

(New Mexico Humanities Review)

ENDANGERED SPECIES

MOTHER/GRANDMOTHER sits alone in the back bedroom.

From her window the burned-out grass is the color of straw and the sick leaves of the elm trees are gray with dust (we have been without rain for ten weeks, the entire middlewest is slowly burning to death) but she thinks she sees the Chesapeake Bay. She has been listening to the reports of the chemicals that were dumped into the James River and she has been thinking constantly of the poisoned fish (she remembers fishing as a child in the clean headwaters of the James . . . Bull Pasture, Cow Pasture, Calf Pasture . . . was it last week, last year, last century?). She wants to turn off her small t-v set, the news is too painful, but she is too tired to move her wheel chair, and besides she is imprisoned by her restraining belt.

Son!

Her thin voice is penetrating but for the moment I pretend not to hear it. After a moment she bangs her cane on the floor above my ceiling, and I put down the book I am trying to review and go upstairs.

At her door I hesitate. I am filled with pity and at the same time an irritable hopelessness. The commentator continues: conspiracy...charges....Hopewell is dying....the Chesapeake Bay is polluted...

Yes, dear, I say. Is anything wrong?

She turns her faded face to me. Her eyes are filled with tears.

The fish, Edward. All the beautiful fish. Her chin quivers. Dying, all of them. Poisoned. All the beautiful fish.

I rest my hand on her pale blue-veined one; last week we removed her diamond rings and I put them in her safe deposit box at the bank, next month we will have to remove *her* to the retirement home, she is too much for us, the children are afraid of her, they dream up excuses not to go upstairs when they come home from school.

Don't worry, dear, I say. I look out at the burned-out wreckage of our garden, only the myrtle around the patio still slightly green, the fountain turned off and littered with dead leaves and bird droppings (*next year even the trees may die*).

They'll come back, Mother. The fish will all come back. I promise . . . . Her eyes wander, her thoughts are elsewhere, she turns to me with fierce urgency.

Edward. Her once-gentle voice is harsh, harsh as when as a child I came home with bad grades on my report card.

Yes, Mother?

You have changed the wallpaper again. While I slept. Why do you continue to change the wallpaper?

No, Mother, no. It is the same, the wallpaper is the same. Why do you think I have changed the wallpaper?

My voice trails away, I try to hide my hopelessness. She is crying silently, I kiss her check, as dry as paper.

———————

DEAD BIRD IN THE BASEMENT

DEAD BIRD IN THE BASEMENT

"I FORGOT TO TELL YOU on the way back from the airport last night," I said to Miss Peaches as we were having mid-morning coffee on the sundeck. "There was a bird in the basement. The night after you'd gone to Savannah to get your mother into the hospital."

"A bird in the basement?"

"That's right. A *dead* bird. I'd showered and dressed and all that, and was about to leave for the airport, and I closed the door without thinking. . . . I tell you, my heart sank when I heard it click shut behind me."

"I can imagine! . . . I've been intending to get that door fixed for weeks."

"It was like 'The Cask of Amontillado!' I had a minute of real panic. And then the frustration! I *had* to catch that plane or . . . ."

"I should think so." Miss Peaches took a sip of her coffee. "Only that one window there and the old door to the garden bricked up. It's a miracle you were able to get out through that small window." She smiled approvingly. "You're in pretty good physical shape to get through *that* . . . . But what about the bird?"

"I was looking for something, anything, so I could somehow get out the window. I was sure I'd miss the plane. And under one of those beatup old kitchen chairs there was this dead bird."

She wrinkled her nose. "Ugh! A dead bird."

"What a night! And during the hay fever season, too. If it hadn't been for that chair. . . . I just got to the airport on time as it was!"

"I'll call the repair man tomorrow," Miss Peaches said. "I should have had that door fixed weeks ago." She paused, and took another sip of her coffee. "But what about the bird?"

"The bird? Very odd, I must say. Very odd indeed. When I got back from the conference it wasn't there."

"Wasn't there? The bird wasn't *there*?"

"That's right. It was gone. As soon as I got back, the first thing I did was go down to the basement — you can be sure I left the door open *that* time — to throw it out. It wasn't there anymore."

"Not *there*! But that's impossible." She made a wry grimace. "Unless Snipe could have. . . ."

"No, it couldn't have been Snipe. You took him out to the vet's, remember, just before you left."

"You're right. Of course. It couldn't have been Snipe. Are you sure . . . I mean, don't misunderstand me, dear, but you know you must have been in an awful lather, worrying about missing your plane, and having to give a lecture the next day, and everything." She paused and looked at me quizzically. "But are you sure there was a bird in the basement? A *dead* bird?"

"Sure? Of course I'm sure."

"But if it isn't . . . I mean if it wasn't there when you got back." Her voice trailed away, and she carefully set her empty cup in the saucer on the table before her. "It just doesn't make sense."

"I know it doesn't make sense. But there *was* a bird down there!"

"What kind of bird?"

"What *kind* of bird?" I shook my head impatiently. "I have no idea what kind of bird. I'd left my glasses on the kitchen table when I went down to get the whiskey. And it was, uh, on the dried-up side. Like mummified. I couldn't tell *what* kind of bird it was. And I'm not an ornithologist, you know; I wasn't in any mood to examine the thing. All I know is it was a dried-up medium-sized bird. Maybe it had been a robin. Certainly not a jay or a cardinal; there wasn't much color to it. But I couldn't really tell. All I wanted to do was to get out of that damned basement. But what difference does it make anyhow, what kind of bird it was?"

Miss Peaches remained silent for a long moment. "Strange," she said, almost inaudibly.

"It's more than strange, if you ask me. It's weird, that's what it is, weird. It reminds me, uh, of that time with the poltergeist in the kitchen."

"The poltergeist in the kitchen!" Miss Peaches wrinkled her nose, a mannerism I find both attractive and annoying. "Oh, no, dear, it doesn't seem at all similar to the poltergeist in the kitchen, not at all."

"Why not?" I demanded.

"Don't be irritated, dear, but a poltergeist — at least *our* poltergeist . . . . well, that's *quite* different from a dead bird. What I mean, there *must* be a natural explanation for that. A perfectly natural explanation, whereas," she paused, weighing her words carefully. "whereas poltergeists are, well, they just *are*."

"You're right," I admitted grudgingly. "You're quite right. I wonder . . . I wonder if, uh, if maybe Snipe could have killed it."

Miss Peaches made a gagging sound. "Snipe *kill* a bird; She's frightened to death of birds, you know that . . . ever since the starlings went after her last summer. And of course, Frank, remember that she was at the vet's."

"Of course," I said. "Of course she was at the vet's." I picked up my coffee cup. "It's about time to get back to work," I said, and headed for the kitchen door. "I guess we'll never know."

At the sill, I drew back my foot, and my stomach turned over. On the mat, an inch or two from my foot, it lay there, the dried-up, feathered corpse of a medium-sized bird.

———————

LAVINIA

(New Letters)

LAVINIA

I AM HALF ASLEEP in the downstairs bedroom when the telephone rings (Miss Peaches sleeps upstairs during the hay-fever season when I'm awake much of the night, sneezing and blowing my nose). I had drowsed off, apparently, some time during the Boston Symphony's Centennial Broadcast (Serkin, incidentally, had been superb in the Beethoven Third Piano Concerto), and it takes me a minute to come to. Still as much asleep as awake, I fumble for the telephone on the bedside table.

"Could I speak to Eleanor?" Just like that, midnight, no hello or anything, just an unpleasant female voice.

"Eleanor has been living in San Francisco for many years," I reply automatically, and then I hear Miss Peaches' voice on the upstairs phone: "Who's calling?"

The reply is instantaneous: "This is Lavinia."

"Lavinia?" Miss Peaches asks, and then the receiver clicks, harshly, followed by silence.

"Wrong number, I guess," I call to Miss Peaches. "Some nut or something." I take another pill, and soon drowse off.

"Who is Lavinia?" Miss Peaches asks at breakfast that morning.

"I have no idea," I say. "I never heard of her. Eleanor never knew anyone named Lavinia."

"Are you sure?"

"I'm never sure of *anything* during this damned hay fever season," I say. "But as far as I know Eleanor never had any friend named Lavinia. If you hadn't heard her on the upstairs phone, I might think I'd imagined it. I was half-asleep, you know, and I'm usually slightly spacey when I've had any of those pills. But what did you think? Of the voice? It sounded sort of childish."

Miss Peaches shook her head emphatically. "No, it didn't sound like a child's voice to me. A woman's, of course; youngish maybe, but not a child's." She half-closes her eyes. "But not an old person's voice, either."

A shiver flickers up and down my spine. "I'm glad you don't think it was an older person's voice. I'd begin thinking it might have been Mother."

"Your Mother! Good Lord, your Mother's been dead for years!"

"Of course, I know it wasn't. But I'm sure glad you heard it too. Those pills! I'd think I might have been hallucinating." I blow my nose vigorously. "But it did sound a little like Mother."

Again Miss Peaches shakes her head. "I don't think so. Not really. Think hard. Are you sure you didn't recognize the voice. Was there *anything* familiar about it?"

"No, not really. I mean . . .; I just couldn't. It was a neutral sort of voice, really. Maybe. . ., maybe sort of cultivated. Slightly . . . uh . . . pleasant, as a matter of fact."

"No, Bob, I wouldn't call it pleasant. Not unpleasant, but certainly not pleasant!" She pauses, strokes her forehead gently. "A little . . . a little breathy, perhaps."

"Breathy? You're way ahead of me now. What do you mean, breathy?"

"It's difficult to say. Maybe . . . maybe a little odd, rather than breathy, maybe. Even a little sinister, too. Yes, definitely! Sinister."

"You're right, come to think of it. It was a little sinister. The whole thing's weird, if you ask me."

Miss Peaches pours herself another cup of tea. "I think you should call Eleanor."

I start to protest, but she shakes her head. She knows how I dislike making long distance telephone calls. And, besides, Eleanor is older than I, and has a heart condition: high blood pressure, hyper-tension, the works. Actually, she could cork off at any time. I don't admit it even to

Miss Peaches, but I worry about Eleanor considerably, even though we've never gotten along very well. As a matter of fact, for a period of several years I actually disliked her, and we've seen very little of each other since she moved to California.

"Not that I think anything's happened to Eleanor," Miss Peaches is saying, "but I do think it would be good for you to call her. Just to make sure."

"Why don't you call her?"

"I really think you should, Bob. But of course if you don't want to."

So I dial San Francisco, preparing myself to hear her daughter — a really sweet child, if there ever was one — answer the phone and tell me that Eleanor has just dropped dead of a heart attack.

I am greatly relieved to hear her voice. She's not a bad woman, actually, but among other things she talks too much. We come from a family of indefatigable, inexhaustable talkers; when I was a child I was surrounded by relatives who, to use an old-fashioned phrase, could talk the balls off a brass monkey, and it is several minutes before I can get to the point.

"Eleanor," I ask. "Did you ever know anybody named Lavinia?"

"Lavinia?" She pauses; I can envisage her sitting in her living room with all the family things, including some very good and extremely valuable water-colors that had belonged to our grandfather, and which I had hoped to inherit; how Eleanor managed to wangle them from the old man I never could figure out . . . .

"Lavinia?" My sister pauses; she is probably examining her long, highly-polished fingernails. "Lavinia? Lavinia? No, Bob, I don't. I never knew anyone named Lavinia. No, never. Why? Why do you ask? I never . . . ."

There is a barely-audible click. The line has gone dead, I think. But then I hear someone breathing. Very heavy breathing. *This is Lavinia, this is Lavinia; let me speak to Eleanor, I must speak to Eleanor. . . . . This is Lavinia. Let me . . . .*

———

THE POLAR BEAR IN THE OZARKS

(Madison Review)

THE POLAR BEAR
IN THE OZARKS

A WARM AFTERNOON in mid-October. We were on our way, Miss Peaches and I, to West Plains. After a warm summer and a cold snap early in October, Southern Missouri was at its best: trees a riot of color, air as sparkling as wine, to coin a couple of phrases. Very few cars on the road. Earlier we had stopped at a small country hotel for one of the best broiled trout we had had in years; they didn't serve wine but we had a jug of chablis in the car and we'd drunk a lot of it with the owner of the hotel, and now I wanted to stretch my legs, walk around a bit and relieve my bladder (we'd left Springfield early that morning, but had stopped frequently, we were in no hurry, we were feeling good). The sun was warm for a late afternoon in autumn, so we drank what was left of the wine. Feeling very good, slightly high.

Back in the car, driving slowly along a winding, slightly-ascending road. Forty or so miles from West Plains. Suddenly my heart lurches. I slam on the brakes, we come to a squealing stop only inches away from a body lying in the middle of the road.

A gigantic polar bear is lying awkwardly in front of us. Parenthetically, I should admit that I have a very good feeling about polar bears. They played a very important part in my life a few years ago; as a matter of fact, a polar bear once almost saved my life. I never, never miss the opportunity to visit the polar bear pits whenever I am near a zoo. Polar bears are full of grace and dignity and, I believe, compassion; I have spent hours sitting in front of the pits at the St. Louis Zoo, the best polar bear pits in the United States: rocky slopes, ledges for sun-bathing, a pool into which they dive with unbelievable grace, agility, and beauty. The poetry of motion! All that enormous strength completely controlled! Beautiful! Should I come back in the form of an animal, I often pray — yes, pray, pray to God Almighty — that it will be in the form of a polar bear. Full of grace, dignity, and — I feel certain — kindness.

But this polar bear does not appear to be full of grace. Almost tragic, his position, lying there on his back, not enjoying the sun as I have seen them do so many times, but almost as though he is in pain.

Cautiously, I switch off the ignition.

Be careful, Miss Peaches is saying, and then, simultaneously, we draw in our breath in amazement.

The polar bear is wearing shoes!

Yes, on his hind paws. (The front paws are unshod).

Gingerly, I get out of the car. The bear raises a massive, black- nailed paw. Slowly and seemingly painfully, he swings his beautiful head towards me.

Aghast, I am frozen in my tracks.

The bear is wearing *my* shoes.

On the left hind paw, a desert boot I had bought in Emporia, Kansas, some years ago when I had gone to the College to give a reading.

On the right hind paw, a Wallaby, darker than the desert boot (and slightly larger, too. . I bought the Wallabys in London last summer...they had always been a little too large for me whereas the desert boots had always been not quite large enough, so I always wore thin sox with the desert boots and heavy sox with the Wallabys).

The bear's shoes are *unmistakably* mine.

I approach the animal gingerly.

Be careful, Miss Peaches says again.

Please to stay behind, I say, I'll be very careful. Please to get into the car, close and lock the door, and roll up the windows.

I continue my approach. Very cautious, searching for the bear's eyes, on the alert for any sudden movement, but my caution and apprehension are fading. By the time I am within a few feet of him, all my fear vanishes. His beautiful eyes meet mine; they do not waver or turn away like the eyes of all other beasts when confronted by a two-legged animal's gaze.

I am within a few feet of him — less than that, I should say, about a foot would be more accurate — when it happens. His eyes are not only kind but *full of recognition*, real recognition.

I kneel down by the poor, shod feet, unlace the shoes, and oh so carefully and gently remove them; suddenly, to my surprise and discomfort, something happens: a great golden arc of urine stains the white fur of the bear's belly and his upper hind legs.

I step back quickly, of course, but not quite quickly enough . . . With great agility, no longer awkward or in pain, the bear rises to his feet and without a backward glance lopes — how beautifully that animal could lope! — down the road and around the bend.

Back in the car, shaking my head, we drive off.

"What do you make of that?" Miss Peaches asks, carefully avoiding my dampened trousers.

"You've got me," I say. "Best not to think too much about it, I guess."

———